THE DEATH OF WASHINGTON'S DEMOCRACY?

THE DEATH OF WASHINGTON'S DEMOCRACY?

A LOOK INTO AMERICA'S FOUNDATION AND FUTURE

To John Shea

Thanks for the great

neighborhood campaigning!

Enjoy

Nick Lampson

NICK LAMPSON

ISBN-13: 9780692934456
Library of Congress Control Number: **2017912889**
LCCN Imprint Name: **Beaumont, TX**

CONTENTS

DEDICATION

Dedicated to my grandchildren: Nicholas, Joseph, Olivia and Jack Shanning and Caroline and Julianna Gertz who I hope will be inspired to continue some of the work I have done in the course of my lifetime promoting civility and the search for common ground.

ACKNOWLEDGEMENTS

I can't express my appreciation strongly enough to my wife Susan, my daughters, Hillary Shanning and her husband Mark, and Stephanie Gertz and her husband Ryan, as well as my brothers and sisters John (JJ) Lampson, Jimmy Lampson (deceased), my hero Mary Jo Lampson Broussard Ford, Gene Lampson and Frances Lampson Breaux, all for believing in me even when we may have had disagreements, and for supporting me through all my many years of political action.

I want to thank my late mother, Nancy Jebbia Lampson, for giving me my smiling personality, my persistence and a strong belief in education; Tahir Javed, CEO of Riceland Healthcare and my employer, for encouraging me and for allowing me time during our business days to complete this book; my colleagues at Riceland Healthcare and CIA retiree Cissie Owen, my assistant Sulyn Hale, Sanaa Hazratjee, Vanessa Vo, Holle Leger for her work designing the book cover, and Shuja Mohammad, for all the work they did in putting the book together, communicating with our publisher and marketing it to the country; to Carrie Chess my congressional science advisor; and to Kathy Travis a retired congressional staffer and author, and Clay Robison a retired Houston Chronicle reporter, for their technical assistance and not letting me drop this project.

Were it not for them, and the friends I have gained all over America and abroad, I would not have had the strength to stay in public life for forty-two years and sacrifice my opportunities to achieve the financial success my family would liked to have had. I didn't want them, or anyone for that matter, to experience any of the ugliness that came along with my public service because I might have had a different opinion than someone with whom I went to church, worked, or lived with in community. I want for them the respect and consideration of any beliefs or suggestions they may have in their attempt to make our community a better place in which to live.

Much of my work, and much of the political crassness which so often today goes along with public service and discourages many to offer themselves for public service, was felt much more by them than by me. Too often, they did not feel the praise and appreciation given to me only because I was in front of a magnificent congressional staff always working in the background to make their "boss" look good. I always wanted those pushing me to feel the love and appreciation that I felt as I sought to help one more person with a problem or strived to receive one more vote.

I hope you enjoy my stories and also feel my concern for the future of our democratic republic and have the courage to speak out and speak up for the goodness that is in every citizen and every community in the United States of America.

May God bless you all.

PREFACE

My childhood in Southeast Texas—I was one of six siblings growing up in a two-bedroom, one-bathroom house—taught me the art of working together, pulling together, and recognizing everyone's needs. Without cooperation and compromise, we couldn't have survived the challenges imposed on a working-class family during the Great Depression and its aftermath. And we did more than survive. We were blessed.

Cooperation and compromise also are essential—although on a much larger scale—to the successful work of the United States Congress, that historic lawmaking body that, for better or worse, has a far-reaching impact on our country's well-being as well as our own everyday lives.

Yet, when I was first elected to Congress in the mid-1990s, the institution was barely functioning. Cooperation and compromise, which historically had overcome partisanship when the nation's welfare was on the line, had broken down in the face of dysfunctional hyperpartisanship that was plunging Washington into gridlock. I thought often of a family member giving up his or her turn in the bathroom when a need arose. If we'd acted the way Congress was, though, there would have been a lot of angry knocks and anxious pacing in the hallway outside the bathroom. I soon launched my own small campaign to change that culture while working as a moderate and consensus-builder on behalf of my Southeast Texas congressional district.

That campaign was temporarily derailed but was soon to become a near obsession after I and several of my fellow Democratic colleagues in the U.S. House of Representatives were dropped into the center of the storm during the mid-decade redistricting scheme carried out in Texas and the federal courts from 2003 to 2005. It was an extraconstitutional power grab designed by then House majority leader Tom DeLay and carried out by Governor Rick Perry and other Republican leaders in my home state. It was ugly, and it was the antithesis of the civility that democracy and representative government need in order to work. It couldn't have been more different from the values my family had instilled in me and my experiences growing up.

My 2001 district in Southeast Texas was radically redrawn in 2003, transformed by the Republican-dominated Texas Legislature into a district with such a significant majority of traditional Republican voters that a Democrat, even an incumbent, could not win. The new district also all but destroyed the influence my hometown, Beaumont, had in Washington. I refused to back away from the political challenge and ran for reelection in 2004 anyway but narrowly lost to the Republican candidate, a very conservative state district court judge from Houston, Ted Poe.

This is a story about my life of public service, the historical mid-decadal Texas redistricting saga, and the bare-knuckled tactics and ethical lapses contributing to Tom DeLay's rise and fall. The story doesn't stop there but has had far-reaching effects, all the way to the present and one of the most unusual presidential elections in our history.

It also is a story about the culture of Congress, how it has been radicalized by redistricting plans, such as the one engineered in Texas by DeLay, that have transformed the vast majority of congressional districts into solidly Republican or Democratic bastions. The result has been the election of increasing numbers of hyperpartisan members to Congress, widening the gulf between the two major parties, routinely turning policy discussions into partisan fighting and, in the process, destroying public service in America.

Small wonder that it took so long for Congress to complete work on such a basic human need as health-care reform only to have, at the first opportunity caused by changing party control, an attempt to repeal and replace the work that had been put in place by the previous majority. The moderate lawmakers so essential to compromise and effective solutions, the kind of statespersons of both parties who helped carry the day for such major legislation as the landmark civil rights laws of my early lifetime, are a vanishing species.

There are other obstacles to restoring cooperation and civility in Washington, DC including the polarizing effects of cable television and talk radio, helped along by government deregulation in the mid-1980s and the 2010 United States Supreme Court decision known as Citizens United, which some speculate could have been ghostwritten by the ethically challenged Tom DeLay, opening the floodgates to corporate spending in political races.

But we can start healing this breach by making sure more congressional districts are truly competitive in the general election, winnable by moderate candidates of either party willing to eschew red-meat partisan rhetoric in favor of negotiation and compromise for the public good. To do that, we must convince our representatives in Congress and statehouses around the country to reform the redistricting process, beginning with the next redistricting year.

That task won't be easy because both major parties will oppose anything that threatens to reduce their clout. But the present system simply isn't working for the American people, and proposed reforms, if given a chance, could help put Congress back on track to civility, real problem-solving for the people, and moving our United States of America forward.

ONE

THE CHANGING WORLD OF U.S. POLITICS

"What in the world just happened?" my daughter rhetorically shouted into the phone to me in a frightful voice. "Dad, can this really be happening?"

The results of the election changed abruptly after we had gone to sleep the night before. The morning of November 9, 2016, brought amazing reaction from across the world, the media, and the political spectrum.

Donald Trump, a self-proclaimed billionaire with no government experience, espousing an extreme right-wing ideology based on an anti-immigrant, racist, and geographical-isolationist platform, was elected president—at least by the electoral college. The U.S. presidential election is always decided by the electoral college, and even though Donald Trump lost the popular vote by about three million votes, the highest losing number of votes in the history of the United States, he still became the president of the United States of America. I had no good answer for my daughter's question, but I felt a great need to try. All I could do then was to reply with this question: "How did we get to this point?" I felt compelled, however, to get an answer and hoped it would include a new direction for our fragile democratic experiment.

Something has changed drastically in this country, and it surely didn't happen overnight. A huge number of our citizens have become alienated from government, from politics, and from one

1

another. They are angry and are not quite sure exactly why. They feel betrayed by the ideal of the American dream, which is not working for them. Each generation is supposed to be more successful, better educated, and have an easier life than the one before it, but that's not happening anymore.

Our social institutions are broken: politics, the economy, education, health care, and more. Even our infrastructure, so necessary to business, commerce, and our way of life, is crumbling around us.

Instead of taking responsibility for these problems, many only look for others to blame. Trump has provided several scapegoats from which to choose: Democrats, liberals, Muslims, and illegal immigrants being his go-tos. This only serves to further divide the country and to provoke more violence.

Perhaps we shouldn't be surprised as the government itself has provided the example of division and partisan factions. It used to be that both parties, especially the moderates in each one, would work together in the spirit of compromise for the good of the entire country. Unfortunately, that is no longer the case. Now, many legislators are not even speaking to one another and seem to have forgotten why they were elected. The phrase "as above, so below," which has been used in relation to the world of magic, comes to mind. I knew there was no magic in what was happening. If the world is changing, it is by someone's design. In relation to our world of politics, how were things before, and how are things today?

Our system of political parties has changed over the course of our history, and it is important for us to recognize warnings given to us by our founding fathers. President George Washington at his farewell address cautioned us to not allow political parties to become more important than Congress:

2

However [political parties] may now and then answer popular ends, they are likely in the course of time and things, to become potent engines, by which cunning, ambitious, and unprincipled men will be enabled to subvert the power of the people and to usurp for themselves the reins of government…which have lifted them to unjust dominion… The common and continual mischiefs of the spirit of party are sufficient to make it the interest and duty of a wise people to discourage and restrain it. It serves always to distract the public councils, and enfeeble the public administration. It agitates the community with ill-founded jealousies and false alarms; kindles the animosity of one part against another; foments occasionally riot and insurrection, and opens the odor to foreign influence and corruption, which find a facilitated access to the government through the channel of party passions.[1]

George Washington did not believe that political parties were good for America and refused to be a part of them. He feared that people would misuse them to gain personal power and to rule over them. They would serve to divide the people rather than unite them, and he was right.

The two major parties are at each other's throats, bringing government almost to a standstill, and the American people are stuck in the middle. It is a tug-a-war for total control of the political system. House and Senate members are closer to enemies than colleagues these days, and we are all suffering for it.

We have achieved gridlock for most legislation, with many legislators not even speaking to those from the other party. It has degenerated into a serious "us versus them" situation and is affecting all issues.

---

1   "George Washington on Political Parties," Victor Daniels, Victor Daniel's blog, ConciousnessandCulture.Com/June 28, 2014, http://consciounessandculture.com/george-washington-political-parties/

We are living examples of what Washington cautioned us not to become. We must change the way we operate our democracy, or we will lose it.

Our country thrived quite well during its first two-hundred-plus years through compromise and the attempt to always find common ground on difficult issues. That respectful means of working together began to disappear with the so-called conservative movement of the 1970s and 80s. That movement began with several Republicans realizing that the Democratic Party had been in power for many years without interruption. Following Barry Goldwater's loss for the presidency and the Watergate fiasco, several conservative think tanks began to be developed, organizations dedicated to developing, promoting, and teaching the principles and ideals of conservatism. Prior to that, there had not been a great deal of information designed specifically to support conservative claims made by politicians promoting issues from the right of the political spectrum.

The first such organization came to be known as the Heritage Foundation. According to Sean Hannity, a radio talk-show host, "No organization on earth is a better supplier of innovative, conservative ideas grounded in the founding principles than Heritage."[2] Hopeful politicians were courted and won over by those espousing these ideals, and these organizations soon began to develop strategies to elect more Republicans to carry their beliefs and to change policy in the government. There were overarching issues such as smaller government, less intrusion of government into our lives and business, and deregulation of many of the controls that had been put in place over many decades, largely by a Democratic majority in the effort to protect and grow a strong middle class in America.

One of the players who was prepared for a role in this new

2   "About Heritage," Sean Hannity, Heritage Foundation, About Heritage, February 2017, https://heritage.org/about-heritage/iimpact

conservative movement was a media consultant, Roger Ailes, who worked on the Richard Nixon and Ronald Reagan campaigns for president. President Reagan brought Roger Ailes into his administration as an adviser in the White House. President Reagan's interest in deregulating government was partly facilitated by the efforts of Roger Ailes. The antitrust laws affecting ownership of media were changed by repealing restrictions that had prohibited mass ownership of media in what had been a successful effort to prevent a monopoly in our free press. Prior to 1987, it was illegal for a person to own interest in more than five radio stations. Each of those radio stations was required to reach out to the general public on an annual basis to survey the kind of effect the radio station was achieving in supporting public information and public activities of the communities served by the station. With the fast changes in technology bringing us computer-driven communications capabilities, some saw the opportunity to change the way messages could be developed and disseminated to the American populace. No one at the time seemed to think of the potential for a very small number of people to craft messages that could then be spread across the United States of America instantly. The feeling was that if the press is free, anyone and everyone can compete to get messages out to the public. Perhaps that idea works well with a few well-placed and crafted controls, but those controls were eroding. Not only did the repeal of the antitrust laws affect media dissemination, but Federal Communications Commission rules dealing with truth in advertising and equal time were changed as well, allowing less accountability for the information that was hitting our airways across America. No longer was it required that information stated over our media outlets had to be truthful and accurate. It was assumed inaccuracies would be corrected by anyone with similar capabilities. It was also assumed that we would continue to have in our society well-trained, ethical journalists whose primary goal was to prepare a well-informed populace. But others could see the opportunity to benefit personally using such magnificent and open airways to promote their political interests. With an FCC that no longer had the legal ability to fully scrutinize and sanction improper use of publicly owned airways, and with the creation of a set of political ethics to "win at any cost," our political landscape could be easily changed, and it was.

Soon after President Reagan's term was over in the White House, his communications director, Roger Ailes, took his media experience and expertise back into the marketplace. According to biographer Gabriel Sherman, author of Roger Ailes's biography, *The Loudest Voice In The Room*, "Roger Ailes revolutionized American politics and media and became the most influential Republican in American life over the last 40 years for figuring out that television and politics were going to become one and the same thing....he learned the techniques of show business and communication as an effective tool of political messaging."[3] He further wrote, "It seems inevitable that Donald Trump has become the Republican nominee as a reality TV star because he is the conclusion of all the work that Roger Ailes has done injecting right wing populism through moving images on television."[4]

In an interview on National Public Radio, Sherman was asked whether it was Ailes's intention to use the Fox News network as a tool for influencing Republican politics and specifically bringing conservatives to power. His response, as reported on NPR was:

3   Michel Martin, "The Rise, Fall, and Lasting Influence of Roger Ailes," *NPR: All Things Considered,* July 23, 2016.

4   Ibid.

"Without question, he (ran) Fox News as a cult of personality. And he believes deep in his heart, as he said to people many times, that he intends to save America, that Fox News was his megaphone to change and save America and preserve the republic."[5]

Sherman continues:

"What Roger Ailes did when he created Fox News was to create a television news network that was anti-journalism. And so what he did with Fox News was to create it as a political campaign that would run against the American media, that would convince millions of Americans not to trust the mainstream—so-called mainstream media, and that Fox News would be the only place on television where you could find the truth. It was a brilliant marketing and political message that created a loyal core of viewers, and so the impact that it's had on American life over the last 20 years is almost impossible to overstate."[6]

All of these changes in the media had affected me and my decades of political action in Southeast Texas. I watched attitudes toward politicians and techniques in campaigning change largely for the worse. Sensationalism and distrust were becoming the rule of the day at that time and into the present. It became harder to find people interested in helping me run for office and in helping people seek public office through public service themselves. Maybe the answer to my daughter's question that had eluded me was coming together. As I thought about these changes I realized that the change in America over the last few decades happened because some strong-believing people saw a different America than I. For most of

---

5   Ibid.

6   Ibid.

my life I wanted to be a public servant and thought I could best serve through elected office. I wanted my children and grandchildren to have the same kind of America in which I grew up. If the conservative movement could change America in the way it did, I now know it is time for us all to band together and change it back. I saw a great society develop in the 1950s with a strong and prosperous middle class and few people at the ends of the wealth spectrum of our country. Today we see that almost all of the prosperity of our nation is held in the hands of only 10 percent of our population. The following chart from 2016 put out by the Federal Reserve[7] shows clearly the position we have reached.

---

7   Federal Reserve Survey of Consumer Finances, February 28, 2017, www. federalreserve.gov

THE DISTRIBUTION OF WEALTH IN THE UNITED STATES

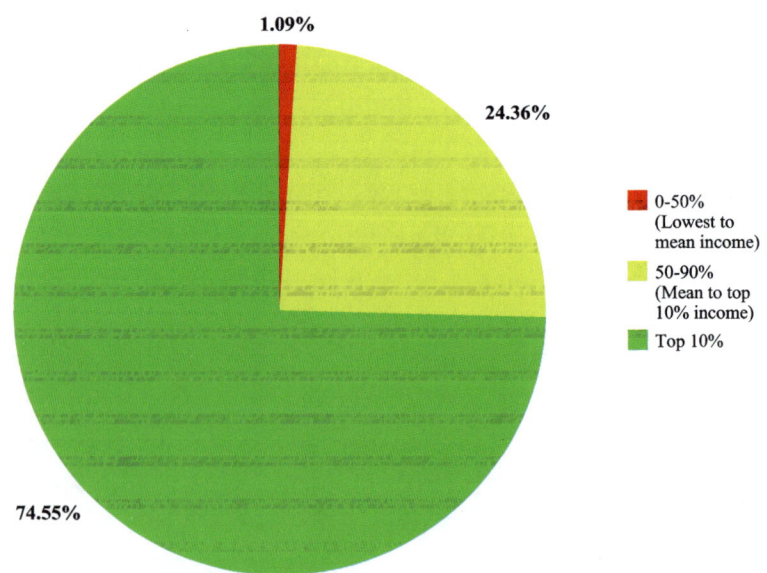

Federal Reserve Survey of Consumer Finances

THE DEATH OF WASHINGTON'S DEMOCRACY?

Regardless of where you are on that chart, future generations of your family will be affected mostly adversely by the reality that is expressed. There are few, if any, people in the middle class, and many of my friends and I are struggling more than we have for decades. I had always been taught that our goal as a democracy was to have great strength in the hands of the masses and not concentrated in the hands of the few. Monetary strength in the hands of small numbers of people as we have seen occur, can subvert the voices of the masses who have less wealth overall. Those voices supported with great wealth are capable of having greater access to media which can set them up as special interests with the ability to influence legislation and thereby present the opportunity to further benefit themselves over those who have less.

Along the way we have seen our political parties change as well. Under the administration of Ronald Reagan, and in his efforts to deregulate government, more laws were changed to further strengthen two major political parties within the government, compounding the competition between them. This was in direct contradiction to what President George Washington asked of us and warned against in his farewell address. Somehow we have to recognize fully what hyperpartisanship and the lack of honest competition between the parties—coupled with changes in how we fund our political parties— is doing to us as a nation and as a democracy. Remember, it was George Washington who asked us not to strengthen political parties for fear they would become more important than Congress, and it was Ronald Reagan who ushered in funding for the two major parties within the federal budget. That alone set up an increase in the desire to control the speakership of the House and helped bring about the division that has, in turn, brought us the congressional gridlock President Washington had warned us to guard against.

We must also remember that the Supreme Court matters, and matters greatly. Hyperpartisanship and the attitude of "win at any cost" have now crept into Supreme Court decisions as well. Extreme partisans put forth Supreme Court nominations as one of the strongest reasons to elect their choice of president. The hyperpartisanship following the election of 2016 has seen the change of long-standing rules in the Senate, which will now change the dynamics of senatorial elections and further divide our country.

As the Supreme Court becomes more partisan because of the influence of presidential elections, decisions such as Citizens United become more likely. Citizens United which was a decision made by the Supreme Court in the name of freedom of speech, in my opinion, restricts speech. It is a decision that allows corporations to give unlimited and unreported amounts of money to political efforts that influence elections. While the Supreme Court's reasoning allowed corporations to exercise free speech, the fact that there is a great deal of unreported money actually stifles speech. Few citizens in the United States of America have the financial wherewithal to compete against the financial power of the super wealthy and corporate interests of this nation. As long as they can use their wealth to influence decisions that help them and leave those who have little to fend for themselves, then we continue to build a system where the rich get richer and the poor become poorer. These are not the values of the great democratic republic envisioned by George Washington and in which I grew up. And it is not a system that I want my children and grandchildren to inherit.

Today, politics is all about the money candidates can raise. When I first went to the DCCC, the Democratic Congressional Campaign Committee, I was told that if I really wanted to win the congressional seat I would be seeking, I needed to do ten things.

The gentleman proceeded to hold up ten fingers and started with number one. He said, "Raise money." Numbers two through nine were exactly the same thing—raise money, raise money, raise money. Number ten he said doesn't count. I got the message. Many others can't and don't.

I have also come to realize the effects of technology in politics. Whether technology affects our ability to get entertainment news as created by Roger Ailes twenty-four hours a day or whether it is an ability to craft congressional districts by leaders like Tom DeLay that will guarantee the election of a specific party, it weakens the ability of the word of the people to be heard in the governance of our country. Citizens must be able to choose their representatives, not the other way around, as we are doing today.

Compounded together, these several facts are taking away the ability of our citizens to make good, thoughtful decisions, which have been the benchmark of success for our country. As citizens hear a continuous stream of political opinions coming from the political left or political right, they are at risk of being brainwashed by the barrage of so-called alternative facts and misinformation. We are then left with electing the followers of the most powerful special interests, not the interests of a knowledgeable, thoughtful, and inclusive electorate. The extremism we have promoted has brought us to a difficult time in our history, wondering what our future might hold. It has left us knowing that if we elect the most liberal liberal and the most conservative conservative, we will never find the middle of the political spectrum where the decisions about important issues affecting our lives and our families will be made.

To me this is the answer to my daughter's question. The question that should now be at hand is where do we go from here? We never know where we're going unless we know where we have been. I will now try to explain the life and experiences that I have enjoyed in my years of politics and put it in context with the question of where we will go next. I believe our country goes through cycles, and this is one of our low points. To start the climb to the next high point, we must realize that moderation is our saving grace, not extremism.

TWO

INTERNING AND DREAMING

I had just witnessed my political career being destroyed before it ever had a chance to begin. Or so I feared after my first encounter with a crusty former World War II marine and legendary congressman from Texas named Jack Brooks.

It was the spring of 1969. I had graduated the previous year from what then was called Lamar State College of Technology (now Lamar University) in my hometown of Beaumont and had just completed my first year of graduate school at Trinity University in San Antonio. I had been a successful student politician in college, had even met then governor John B. Connally, who gave me some helpful political advice, and now I was campaigning hard for a summer internship in Brooks's congressional office in Washington. Maybe too hard.

Brooks was my congressman. I had never met him, but I had applied the year before for the Lyndon Baines Johnson Student Internship in his office and been turned down. The competition for the plum opportunity was stiff, and I was determined not to lose out this time. I had heard that the intern selected for Brooks's office the previous year had submitted more than the three requested letters of recommendation, and I was not going to be outdone.

I spent several months researching financial contributors to Brooks's political campaigns, visiting them, and requesting letters on my behalf. Nearly all were happy to help out a local kid, so I was able to compile a small mountain of favorable letters in the congressman's office by the time I finally had a chance to meet the Honorable Mr. Brooks in person.

I went to Groves, Texas, where Congressman Brooks and U.S. Senator Ralph Yarborough were scheduled to dedicate a new post office. I got there bright and early, making sure I did not miss an opportunity to walk up and introduce myself. I was feeling confident that my chances of getting selected this time were good, but I figured they would be further improved if the congressman actually met me.

It was raining, and when they arrived, Brooks and Yarborough walked quickly up the sidewalk to get inside. But ignoring the weather and my own common sense, I stood in the middle of the sidewalk, blocking their way. As the congressman approached, getting wetter with each step, I stuck out my hand and eagerly and confidently announced, "Mr. Brooks, I am Nick Lampson."

Despite the rain, he stopped abruptly, his face turning into the famous scowl that I was to see many more times over the course of my relationship with him. He stepped up close to me, well inside my personal space—his time-honored intimidation tactic—and, without shaking my outstretched hand, growled menacingly, "You send me one more g-d—m letter and I will throw your whole f—k-ng file in the garbage can!"

He pushed me off the sidewalk and brushed past me into the building. Stunned and mortified, I almost cried. My whole political future had just evaporated, and I was devastated.

After the initial shock, I realized that Congressman Brooks at least knew my name. Nevertheless, I worried for days that I had blown my chance to spend the summer in Washington working as an intern in the U.S. House of Representatives. Although I knew the congressman's friends had said nice things about me—and in politics you listen to your friends—his harsh, profane reaction had shaken me to the core.

Brooks let me stew for about a month, but then I got the call for which I had been working for so long. June 1969 was an extraordinary time in our nation's life, and it was a great time for a twenty-four-year-old kid from Beaumont, Texas, to be in Washington, DC.

President Johnson, a Democrat from Texas, had left office only a few months earlier, turning the White House over to Republican Richard Nixon. But Democrats still controlled the House of Representatives, and Jack Brooks was chairman of the powerful Government Operations Committee, which he ran in the style he had been taught by his Texas friends, LBJ and Mr. Sam—the late Sam Rayburn, the former longtime Speaker who had ruled the House with a heavy but productive hand.

Even today, members of the Texas Democratic congressional delegation talk with reverence of the storied "Board of Education" room in the U.S. Capitol, where Mr. Sam and his Democratic team would twist arms and otherwise "educate" wayward colleagues about the wisdom of supporting the Speaker's priorities. Poker and whiskey were part of the standard team-building curriculum.

A frequent visitor to the small room, located in a corridor along the south end of the Capitol, was Harry S. Truman, first as a member of Congress from Missouri and later as vice president. Truman was in the "Board of Education" room with the Speaker that historic day in 1945 when he received a phone call from First Lady Eleanor Roosevelt informing him that President Roosevelt had died and he was now in charge of ending World War II.

My boss and teacher, Jack Brooks, first elected in 1952, was an institution on Capitol Hill. He was rough and gruff and thoroughly intimidated almost everyone around him, as I had learned the first time I met him. But as much as he was feared, he also was much loved, although only by those who knew him well or not at all. He was referred to by many names. His favorite, however, was "Mr. Chairman." No one called him Jack except his beloved Charlotte. I always referred to him as "Congressman." And some called him SOB…Sweet Old Brooks, of course.

This U.S. Marine veteran of World War II combat in the Pacific was nearly unable to finish a sentence without saying the f-word. On the desk in his Capitol office sat his nameplate, his name facing visitors. On the back, the side facing him, were the words "No Cussing."

But Brooks couldn't be tamed, and none of us who worked for him really wanted him to be, because you can't corral a wild mustang. Chairman Brooks always went his own way.

Within a few years, during the 1974 impeachment proceedings after the Watergate scandal, Brooks would draft the historical articles of impeachment against President Nixon. After Nixon resigned, Brooks had a beer but wouldn't celebrate.

Brooks was a strong Democrat who on countless occasions eagerly voted against Republicans. But he also was part of the most important bipartisan effort of my lifetime, the enactment of the landmark Civil Rights Act of 1964. He also supported the Voting Rights Act of 1965. Neither piece of legislation, strongly opposed by most Democratic congressmen from the South and many of their constituents, would have passed without the leadership of President Johnson and the strong support of non-southern Democrats and Republicans.

When necessary for the sake of their country, congressional Democrats and Republicans of that era could put partisan differences aside. I shudder to think what would have happened to civil rights legislation if today's Republicans and Democrats in Congress, who can hardly agree on anything, had been in office then. I also shudder to think about not having the memories of my brothers and sisters and neighborhood friends playing "Mother May I" in our front yard well into each summer night in Southeast Texas and the camaraderie with which we grew up. It is too bad that those childhood games are not required experiences for service in our Congress.

The summer of my internship was the summer of my life. Intern duties varied from office to office. I did research, operated automatic typewriters (which were state of the art at the time), covered committee hearings that other staff members were unable to attend, and had the run of the whole Capitol.

One of my favorite duties was taking constituents on tours, making new friends and telling them stories of our history, as laid out in the rooms, paintings, and statues throughout the historic building. Internships on the Hill are an amazing opportunity for young people who want to see how laws are made. Interns also have opportunities to forge lifelong connections; meet celebrities, politicians, and world leaders; and watch history being made from backstage.

I once sat three rows behind President Nixon at a Washington Senators baseball game at RFK stadium. That seemed to be no big deal in those days of less worry and lower security. The Watergate scandal, which later would dog Nixon, hadn't yet erupted.

People could still easily get a public tour of the White House and could walk unimpeded into and out of the Capitol. One day, I sat and listened in the Senate chamber to Senator Everett Dirksen, a Republican from Illinois and in my opinion one of our greatest statesmen, debate an issue with a young Teddy Kennedy. Dirksen's raspy voice will never leave my memory.

We interns formally met from time to time to hear from members of Congress or representatives of the administration. We also attended receptions at foreign embassies, where we often felt like junior diplomats of some sort, talking about our country with people from other nations.

Sometimes, we were invited to late suppers, where power brokers often determined the course of laws they soon would pass. I remember meeting the then emperor of Ethiopia, Haile Selassie, at a reception in the lobby of the White House. That meeting made a particularly huge impression on me when months later I learned that he had put his own son to death for trying to overthrow his government. That action made me appreciate all the more the way our civil government works. I also recall roaming the grounds of the Chinese embassy at an afternoon reception for government employees. That was around the time that President Nixon was planning his historical trip to China. Many years later I had the opportunity to view Polaroid photographs thumbtacked to the walls of Chairman Mao Tse-tung's home in China depicting President Nixon's visit there. The experiences I was living and the diverse people and interests I had the pleasure of enjoying made an impression on me that would affect the way I would live my life forever.

All in all, it was a great—and heady—experience. Maybe, sometimes, a little too heady.

On a dare, I once tried to call Tricia Nixon, the president's older daughter, to ask for a date. I got as far as her personal secretary before being turned down. I still think she would have liked me.

I loved to go to the slope around the Washington Monument, sometimes with a date, and have wine and cheese and bread and just stare at the stars and the magnificent surroundings. It was thrilling to imagine what had happened in that very spot over the course of history and to feel a part of it, even as a lowly intern.

I also dwelled on what kind of role I might someday play in our country's history. Our federal government worked then because lawmakers from both parties knew when to cooperate and compromise, and that summer had built the confidence of an impressionable young man who started to think he could change the world.

I would return to Washington and Congress twenty-eight years later, but I would find a different place.

THREE

IT TAKES A TEAM

My family story, like that of so many others, is a tapestry of immigration—the beginning of new lives and hopes in the United States. Both sets of my grandparents came to Texas from Sicily a century ago. I am sure they never dreamed that one of their grandsons would someday serve in the United States Congress, but they came with the sheer will to build their own American dream in their new world.

My mother's parents were married in a little Catholic church in Alcamo, Sicily. My grandmother traveled across the Atlantic by herself as a young teenage bride to join her husband in the United States of America. My father's parents married in a church in New Orleans, Louisiana, after they arrived from Poggioreale, Sicily, and Salemi, Sicily. Both couples settled in Stafford,Texas in Fort Bend County, raised their children on adjacent farms, and founded a church that still stands today. The predecessor of today's Holy Family Catholic Church in Missouri City, it reflected the image of the changing immigrant nation that the United States was becoming.

My grandparents experienced the emotional rewards of living a life with abundant mutual respect and appreciation for their neighbors. They left this world without ever tasting the worldly delights of which they had dreamed. But they certainly blazed a path for their legacy in the generations to come, something I was to realize many years later as I stood in the United States House of

Representatives, taking my oath of office for the first time. My heart soared with the appreciation that I was living my grandparents' dream—and the dream of millions of other immigrants—for life, liberty, happiness, and success in America.

My five siblings and I spent a lot of time on our grandparents' farms. We were free labor, picking cotton and okra. We weren't very good at it and didn't pick very much, but we learned invaluable lessons. Toiling in the sun gave us the perspective of those who struggle to eke out a life from the soil.

Grandpa Jebbia, my mother's father, was a very religious man. He depended on his prayers and his faith to help him take care of his family, to provide for all their needs—food, shelter, education, and even medical care. They didn't have health insurance in those days. When someone was sick, everyone prayed very hard for his or her recovery.

They had little more than hard work and their belief that they would be OK, that their family would survive and life would get better. That belief was central to their family dynamic and was passed on to the next generations.

My parents grew up, met, and married in Fort Bend County. My father, Julius, managed a small grocery store owned by the Court family in Stafford, and my mother, Nancy, helped him in the store and took care of their apartment upstairs. My two oldest brothers were born while they lived there.

My parents began their married life during the Great Depression, when thousands of American families did everything and anything to live to see the next day. My older brother, J. J., told of a time when he opened the door of the house in which my parents were living in Stafford to let in the liquor revenue agents as my mother was pouring Daddy's handiwork, a batch of moonshine, down the drain.

Illegal though it was, moonshine provided a marketable use for corn crops after corn prices had plummeted. Unfortunately, though, moonshine also provided a false sense of escape from reality for many people struggling through those dark days.

Another story from the late 1930s while they were still living in Stafford that fascinated and frightened us as children was about Daddy being stopped by the police and having no explanation for the 150 pounds of sugar he had in his car. Sugar was rationed in those days, and hoarding sugar was a telltale sign for the liquor police.

Among the many things that Daddy did to scrape together a living during those hard times also included showing movies and even turning a small building he owned with my grandfather into a pool hall. But after too many fights among patrons, and seeing the place torn up too many times, they decided the pool hall was more trouble than it was worth. They gave the place to the Catholic Diocese of Houston Galveston so the community could have a place to worship.

The building that had failed as a pool hall and bar succeeded as a church. After holding services there for many years, the Holy Family Catholic Church moved down the street to its present location.

The final blow for my parents and their young family in Fort Bend County was a fire that destroyed the grocery store and their apartment. They lost everything except their little boys and the clothes they were wearing.

That would be the first of many times that my mother would be heard to say, with tremendous certainty, that something good would come from all the bad that was happening to the family.

Soon after the fire, Daddy, who had only a third-grade education but could speak four languages, got a job selling furniture at the Phoenix Furniture Company in Beaumont. It was an appropriately named employer for a hardworking man who literally was rising from the ashes of his most recent setback.

My parents soon settled into their new community. Four more children, including me, would be born in Beaumont. They bought a small house, and we all enjoyed the beautiful Southeast Texas coast with its rugged legacy of great fishing and hunting. My parents also began to pass on to their children the lessons of determination and hard work they had learned from their own parents.

But the hardships were not yet over. My older sister, Mary Jo, contracted polio. She lived and thrived, but only after a long hospitalization and fierce struggle. And my father soon would be plagued by a series of health problems that would lead to his premature death.

During World War II, the area around Beaumont and Orange became a shipbuilding hub in addition to being a booming center of oil refining. Daddy worked as a welder deep in the bowels of the huge U.S. Navy ships being constructed for the war effort. He did his part to help America win the war but lost his own health in the process, thanks to asbestos exposure. By the end of the war, about the time I was born, he had already spent a year in and out of a tuberculosis hospital. And he suffered from lung and heart problems the rest of his shortened life.

Heroically, he continued to do whatever he could to provide for his family. He sold furniture, Bibles, refrigeration equipment, whatever it took, whatever he could sell. But he passed away when I was twelve. I knew my dad all too briefly, but it was from him that I learned the lessons of a strong work ethic.

Daddy had been the family breadwinner. Now, suddenly, all of us were finding ways to help support the family.

Mom got nineteen dollars a month for each of us from Social Security, so long as all the kids stayed in school and were younger than twenty-one. Soon she took a job as a seamstress for an upscale dress shop in Beaumont, which would provide most of the family income.

About that time, as a twelve-year-old, I got my first job. I emptied garbage cans and swept the gym building at Pietszch Elementary School, where my sister taught. The work wasn't hard, but I had to be there regularly. Mr. Marino, the school janitor, was my boss and taught me many lessons, including how to take and follow instructions.

I also remember collecting soda-water bottles for the two-cent deposit and doing other odd jobs, including delivering groceries on a bicycle for a neighborhood grocer.

We lived in a tiny, two-bedroom wooden-frame house with a screened-in back porch. It had a kitchen, dining room, living room—and one bathroom—for eight people, seven after my father died. Using the bathroom had to be scheduled, but it was amazing how we got along, how we all fit in that small place.

We slept everywhere, including the back porch and the dining room. My younger sister, Frances, and I slept in a bed in our parents' room until J. J. went off to the army. Because of her struggle with the effects of polio, my older sister Mary Jo eventually got the second bedroom all to herself. She had parallel bars there so she could practice standing and walking.

Despite our circumstances, I never thought of my family as particularly poor. The other kids in the neighborhood wore blue jeans with holes in them, just like I did, and that was before wearing blue jeans with holes was considered fashionable. We usually patched our jeans, and we put cardboard or folded paper in the bottoms of our shoes to make them last until Easter. That was the time, once a year, when we got new clothes.

And Mom always seemed to be able every few weeks or so to find enough old clothes to fill a bag for a needy family down the street.

I enjoyed a happy homelife and the typical, simple things of childhood. We played ball, flew kites, raced, climbed trees, and plotted with our friends and siblings. I also joined the Boy Scouts.

My mother, Nancy Jebbia Lampson, had dropped out of school in the fifth grade to work in her family's cotton fields. Yet she knew that a good education was the most valuable tool she could give her children. She made sure that all six of her children graduated from college with at least one degree. And, at age eighty, still going strong, she received her GED to a standing ovation from a crowd of family and friends, and love, pride, and tears from her children.

The education legacy remains strong in the Lampson family. Before I began my pursuit of being elected to public office, I was a high-school science teacher. My wife, Susan, is a special education teacher, and our two daughters are board-certified teachers.

"When there is a will, there is a way" was one of my mother's favorite sayings. It also was how we lived our lives. There was no shortage of will among the Lampsons. And we would find a way, whether it was balancing the family budget, helping my big sister recover from polio, or helping our neighbors in need. Through it all, we were a team.

Family relationships form the foundations of the persons we become. The family is where we learn our people skills, where we learn to be part of a cohesive unit. It is where we begin to learn problem-solving and negotiation, how to transcend differences for the good of the group.

Members of my close family are defined by a set of core values, an uncommon commitment to serving others, a willingness to take on any worthwhile challenge—no matter how difficult—and a determination to see things through.

The strength of a family unit can apply to Congress. If Congress were more conscious of the need to resolve individual and political differences for the greater good, collegiality and friendship could transcend partisanship, and the taxpayers' business could be conducted.

Not too many years ago, Congress operated as a family unit. Members would argue—often heatedly—over their differences but ultimately would negotiate compromises for the good of the country. Congress was still like that during my staff internship as a young man in 1969. But that was before the partisan bomb-throwers brought effective government to a grinding halt.

It is past time to restore collegiality and civility in Washington. The size and diversity of Congress, of course, make problem-solving on Capitol Hill much more difficult than the task faced by most families. But that size and diversity also make the task critical to our country's future. I am so grateful to have been a part of a family who could always decide together what we wanted to eat, who would wash the dishes, who would sweep the floors, who would mow the yard, and who would hang the clothes out to dry on the clothesline in the backyard. It made life so much easier and led to a life of love and respect for one another. Shouldn't our Congress be the same?

FOUR

My Sister, My Hero

My older sister, Mary Jo, was an active fourteen-year-old when she contracted polio in 1949, several years before a vaccine against the devastating disease had been introduced.

Our family's life for the next two years would be centered on John Sealy Hospital in Galveston, where caregivers fought to save her life while my parents fervently prayed that their little girl wouldn't be taken from them. The doctors prepared our family for Mary Jo's likely death, but it didn't come.

The disease left Mary Jo totally paralyzed from the neck down, and she spent much of a year in an iron lung. But the good Lord never took away her breath of life. And Mary Jo was as determined as her parents and her grandparents that this huge hurdle was not going to get the best of her. It never has.

I was only five when Mary Jo contracted polio, and she has been my hero ever since. My earliest memories of our time together were of our family visits to the hospital, where she lived for two years, fighting the ravages of the disease and learning to live despite it.

The whole family went to visit her every weekend, making the sometimes more than two-hour trip from our home in Beaumont down the coast of the Gulf of Mexico and across the Houston-Galveston ship channel by ferry. Our mother brought Mary Jo schoolbooks and lessons from her teachers, and we always had a special outing planned around our visits. Mother would prepare picnic lunches, and Daddy would take us fishing or crabbing, or we would just go to the beach or some other special spot on beautiful Galveston Island. As she regained her ability to breathe on her own, Mary Jo would join us for increasingly long periods away from the hospital.

Despite my sister's hospitalization, these outings were wonderful because the entire family was sharing special time together. I wouldn't leave Mary Jo's side during those visits, and soon I became the "master" of the wheelchair that had become Mary Jo's means of mobility.

The doctors, amazed at the will of the human heart and the strength of the Almighty, finally came to realize that Mary Jo would live. They told my parents that she would be able to return home but probably would be paralyzed and bedridden, with little ability to move her arms or legs, for the rest of her life. And that life, they predicted, probably would be short.

The doctors believed my big sister would never return to school, would not graduate, would not marry or have children or ever be able to support herself.

Nevertheless, Mary Jo's return home after two years in the hospital was a happy day for her family. My parents laid her down on the backseat of the black 1949 four-door Chevrolet for the seventy-mile trip from Galveston, across the Houston-Galveston ship channel by ferry, and through the coastal marshes and rice farms to our house in Beaumont. I sat on the floorboard beside her. Cars didn't have seatbelts in those days, or air-conditioning, but we didn't care. My big sister was coming home!

Once again, the doctors would be proven wrong, thanks to Mary Jo's sheer will, my mother's equally strong determination, and our family's hard work and strong faith.

Mary Jo clearly had inherited her strong will from our mother. From the very beginning, they both refused to accept that she would never walk again. "If you will it, you will do it," Mother believed, and that willpower was contagious. Soon, everyone in the family and our friends were helping Mary Jo strengthen her legs, a huge test that we all had to get through together.

Mary Jo slowly began to strengthen her muscles, which had quit working. She discovered she could lock her knees, so we designed an at-home therapy exercise. Mother would steady my sister on her feet and hold her up while I picked up one foot at a time and moved each one forward to simulate walking.

We did that exercise over and over, every day, every month, until Mary Jo's legs were strong enough to hold her up and move her feet on their own. It was very repetitive, but it was never a chore. In fact, it was fun, and we frequently turned it into a game. As in meeting other life challenges—personal, professional, even political—working together makes all the difference.

Day after day, Mary Jo got stronger. Soon she was strong enough to sit up in her wheelchair, which had been given to her by the March of Dimes. Although she would need to use a wheelchair for the rest of her long life, Mary Jo never let it slow her down. It became a tool for making new friends, a chair with wheels that— after a few minutes of talking with Mary Jo—was invisible.

Thanks to the help of her teachers at South Park High School, who literally made house calls, Mary Jo kept up with her schoolwork at home and graduated on time with her class.

That, in and of itself, was a great accomplishment, particularly in the 1950s, for someone who had been through what Mary Jo had been through. But she was just getting started. Soon, she enrolled at Lamar State College of Technology (now Lamar University) in Beaumont, where she was the only one on campus who moved around in a wheelchair.

Either my brothers or her friends would pick her and her wheelchair up at our house on Elgie Street in the South Park part of Beaumont and take her to Lamar for classes. Once on the campus it was still a chore getting to and from class. There weren't any ramps, mechanized wheelchairs, or other special facilities in those days to give her a break. She couldn't wheel herself around, so, with patience and her pretty smile, she would find someone to push her.

When they got to the steps of a building, Mary Jo and whoever was pushing her would have to enlist help to carry her up, often from young men who couldn't say no to her flirtatious smile. When class was over, there always was someone ready to help her get out of the building and on to her next class.

While in college, Mary Jo began to take art lessons. She started with oils, painting shrimp boats, marshes with ducks, and other Southeast Texas landscape scenes of our youth. Then she began using watercolors, and over her lifetime she became quite an accomplished artist.

Someone always drove her to the places she was interested in painting. She had hundreds of friends who were always there to participate in her activities.

She became so popular in her first year at Lamar Tech that her fellow students elected her homecoming queen in 1952. She was escorted by Lynn Sweat, who later would become a nationally known artist after leaving Southeast Texas and moving to Connecticut.

Mary Jo earned a bachelor's degree from Lamar Tech with majors in commercial art and social science, and she did it in four years. Then she was ready for another challenge.

After a summer at Stephen F. Austin College in Nacogdoches, Texas, she enrolled in a master's program in speech and hearing pathology at the University of Houston—one hundred miles from

Beaumont. This was in 1955, and people in wheelchairs didn't do things like that then. They were "handicapped." Or so other people thought. But Mary Jo was a trailblazer. The wheelchair became her tool to do things faster and better, and we moved her to Houston. Lorella Spalding (now Rivet), Mary Jo's longtime friend, had been with her that summer at Stephen F. Austin and was a huge help to her in getting around. When she went off to the University of Houston, she stayed in the dormitory and was assigned a roommate from St. Louis, Missouri. She did not like her arrangements, and her roommate was always gone with her boyfriend and was not around to help Mary Jo as Lorella had.

One day, when she got just plain homesick, she called the men's dormitory and asked if anyone there was going to Beaumont for the weekend. Joe Broussard came to the phone and said he would pick her up and take her. When he arrived at Mary Jo's dorm, he discovered that "picking her up" was exactly what he had to do; he lifted her out of her wheelchair and put her into his car. Not too many years later, Joe would become my sister's husband and the father of their four children. He was a wonderful husband for her, extremely attentive to her every need. He even built house for her especially adapted to her needs as a wheelchair user and had it ready for her when they got married. It was unfortunate that she lost him to cancer when he was only fifty years old.

Again, Mary Jo did not let her loss get her down. It wasn't long before she met Bob Ford, who was not only perfect for her as a dedicated husband but also as an experienced cowhand who could help her continue to run the cattle farm she and her late husband had started for their children. Mary Jo and Bob Ford still oversee a herd of cattle that exceeds more than four hundred head of mother cows. I told you she is an amazing person!

On finishing her master's degree, Mary Jo returned to Beaumont and began teaching in the South Park Independent School District. During her seven-year teaching career followed by many years of private student therapy sessions in her home studio, she helped hundreds of young and old people with speech or hearing difficulties to live productive lives. She became their hero, too.

While she was still a young schoolteacher, Mary Jo decided she wanted to drive a car and turned to her doctors for help. Doctors in Dallas refused, but her Beaumont doctor agreed. He transplanted a muscle from her right leg to her left foot so she could use that foot to operate the accelerator and the brake. Without ever being able to raise either of her arms—that wasn't necessary to turn the steering wheel—she drove for thirty years and never had a wreck.

Although I was only a teenager at the time, I was among those who taught Mary Jo to drive. I had been given a special exemption from state law to allow me to get my driver's license at fourteen, instead of sixteen, so I could help my "handicapped" sister get to and from work. I was proud of her accomplishment and proud of myself for helping her. And I was thrilled when she went out and bought a brand-new 1959 Thunderbird because I got to drive it. Not bad for a high-school kid who had become accustomed to riding a bicycle to school.

Everyone needs a hero, a role model to look to for guidance, to instill confidence, to show you how to turn seemingly impossible goals into reality. My big sister was my hero, and still is. I learned early on not to tell her she couldn't, because she always showed me that she could. When she reached a point that she could not hold her arm up to a canvas to paint, she would lie down on the bed with her painting and reach the portion of the canvas closer to her hand. She would turn the canvas to reach all areas of it, which meant that she would paint right-side up, upside down, and sideways in order to complete her thought. She showed amazing talent. She also showed true grit when she took on the Jefferson County Commissioners Court in 1974, forcing them to provide a means to allow her and her wheelchair to get into the Jefferson County courthouse to attend the County Commissioners' Court meeting. Their solution to the many barriers between the parking lot and the courtroom was to place a doorbell at the curb that would ring in the maintenance department of the courthouse and summon someone to come, pick up her wheelchair, and carry her into the courthouse. It wasn't the best solution, but it worked until they did something better later on. Nothing would've happened had it not been for her willingness to step up and make a difference.

FIVE

MUSIC, POLITICS, AND TEACHING IN THE WINTER OF SEGREGATION

As a young man in Southeast Texas in the 1960s, I saw the transition from segregation to integration from several perspectives. Perhaps the most memorable was as a young musician. I still believe music was a greater natural integrator of diverse Americans than court rulings.

Growing up in the stomping grounds of Janis Joplin, Edgar and Johnny Winter, and Jerry LaCroix, I loved rhythm and blues and bands with horn sections. I learned to play the saxophone, and by the time I was fifteen, I was good enough to start playing in local bands. It was great fun, and I made a few bucks.

Edgar Winter organized a band called the Soul Counts, and we played nightclubs from Houston to New Orleans. One night, our band, which was all-white, was playing at a black nightclub on Crockett Street in Beaumont. This was quite a novelty for that part of the country during those days, but our band was beginning to do this more and more.

Late that particular night, however, in a crowded ballroom so thick with smoke we couldn't see the other end of the room, one of the revelers pulled out a gun and started shooting holes in the ceiling. My bandmates and I couldn't see the ruckus, but we knew the mood of the times. This was the volatile sixties, when passions over integration were easily inflamed, and we were a bunch of white guys in a black club. We immediately started scrambling out the back door, juggling our horns, guitars, cases, drums, and amplifiers. The club owner was very apologetic later, but we had been very scared.

That was a very unusual occurrence. Generally, the crowds pushed the club owners to have us back for future engagements. We even started seeing some white faces in the crowds of black partiers where we were playing. We had worked at learning the music that came to be known as soul music, rhythm and blues, and blue-eyed soul. Our bands did a good job of emulating the sounds of Ray Charles, Otis Redding, Aretha Franklin, Little Richard, and other popular sixties recording artists. Jerry (Count Jackson) LaCroix was the singer I enjoyed most in our band. Forty years later he still had a following in Southeast Texas and Southwest Louisiana. If anyone ever deserved the title of a blue-eyed soul entertainer, it was Jerry. And with the musical genius of Edgar Winter, we were able to copy the very recognizable and loved sounds of melodic horns, organ, bass, and drums backing up the musical words made popular by black artists. Our mostly white band began to have a following in both the white and black communities.

I believe today that we played a small part in making the music that brought at least some of our racially diverse community together. There was no debate over loving and enjoying that kind of music, and we did it well.

In 1968, the band got a six-week contract to play in Las Vegas. It was my last semester of college, and I had to choose between making music under the bright lights in Sin City or completing work on my degree. I chose to graduate and left the band, some of whose other members went on to do great things in the music and entertainment world. Edgar and Johnny Winter—who ended up in New York—along with Jerry LeCroix did well with a band called White Trash, and Jerry operated a recording studio in Reno, Nevada, for many years before coming back to Beaumont, Orange and Port Arthur, the Golden Triangle of Southeast Texas where he will always be loved and listened to.

I loved those days of playing music and still miss performing today. The thing I was most grateful to learn during those days was the simple truth that white people and black people are divided only by our own prejudices. A band of musicians is much like a family in which the same dynamics of relationship apply. No good-quality music can be created where there is anger, discord, or lack of cooperation. Perhaps our Congress will realize that a little fine-tuning in their relationships might go a long way to restore some semblance of harmony in the legislative branch.

College was an exciting place to be in the sixties. Not only was the civil rights movement running strong, the Vietnam War was also tearing away at the nation's conscience. Emotions about Vietnam ran high on both sides of the issue. We had regular debates as students on the merits of that war. All of my friends had stories of other friends they had lost due to the fighting and constantly questioned why. Many still went over there, and some didn't. We will always remember those who gave all and did not come back, and always respect and appreciate those who went to fight as well as those who chose to stay home. And amid all this history, I was a student politician—and a pretty successful one.

I had gotten my first taste of politics in high school, where I had been on the student council, but my career took off at Lamar. Within a couple of years, I had risen from student representative to president of the student body. I helped organize campus debates over Vietnam, assisted the board of regents in planning a new student center, and organized a student campaign for Beaumont urban renewal.

THE DEATH OF WASHINGTON'S DEMOCRACY?

At a meeting of the Texas State Students Association, where I was elected treasurer, I also met and got to have a short, but memorable, conversation with then governor John B. Connally. There must have been five hundred college kids at that meeting in our state's capital, Austin, and they all wanted to shake the governor's hand. I wanted to do more than shake his hand. I wanted to ask him something. So, I went to the end of a very long line and waited my turn.

When the governor finally got to me, I asked him how he knew what he wanted to be when he grew up. He graciously and patiently told me about his young years and his family's struggles. His early life seemed not too different from my own.

His family had struggled. My family had struggled. Education and hard work had opened the door to a better life for him. My community had given me the same invaluable gifts of education and the opportunity to work.

When Governor Connally told me he had been president of the student government in college and had learned about giving back to his community through public service, I felt as if I had been struck by a thunderbolt. Enough had already happened in my life to make me realize that I shared some of what had made this famous politician who he was. He had a vision for his community, and he had found his way to make a difference.

Governor Connally told me how he had set goals for himself years earlier and had written them down on a piece of paper. He thought he could best give back to his community by holding elected office. His eventual goal was to be governor of Texas, and he had charted a path that included the milestones he thought would be necessary to reach that goal. He said it was important to write the targeted milestones down, to periodically look at them for reinforcement, and to be willing to change direction if new opportunities arose.

The governor didn't tell me about his future plans or goals. I always wondered if he had written down the future cabinet positions he would hold or his later campaign, which fell short, for president of the United States. I would bet he did.

To whom much is given, much is demanded. It doesn't have to be just money. It also can be talent and ability. When we have much, we owe much more to one another. That has become a driving factor in my life.

I left that meeting with Governor Connally and went to my hotel room to write down my life's goals. I have since revised those goals to reach for unexpected opportunities. But I have learned to appreciate the wisdom that John Connally gave me in two areas—plotting a plan and making that plan about something bigger than myself. My list is shorter now but no less important, and even after forty years of running for and holding public office, I still have dreams that need to be accomplished. These are dreams for my family and for my community. They are not any different than the dreams my grandparents held in their hearts and minds when they left their homeland in search of opportunity in that new land known as America. To a large extent my dreams are not as difficult as theirs because they blazed a huge trail for me to follow and opened doors that I would otherwise not have been able to open, but they are no less important. I still must do my part. I understand that change will always begin with me.

After graduating from Lamar in 1968 with a BS in biology and science education, I moved to San Antonio to attend Trinity University's graduate school in hospital administration and to teach school. I taught seventh-grade life science during the day and went to graduate school at night. This was part of my plan, but I really wanted to serve my community in some other way.

I had already learned that helping people was more about putting people together with those who could help, rather than solving each person's problem personally. It came easily to me...the ability to put someone who needed something together with someone who could provide it. There is a solution to every problem if you will but look for it.

I was nearing the end of my summer internship in Congressman Brooks's office in Washington in 1969 and planning to return to graduate school and my teaching job in San Antonio when I learned of another opportunity. There would be an opening for a seat in the Texas House of Representatives from Jefferson County, my home county. A longtime state representative, Jimmy Weldon, who served our community very well, had decided to leave the legislature to run for justice of the peace.

According to my life plan, which I had drafted after meeting with Governor Connally, I would run for a state house seat, but not until I was thirty-five. At this time, I was only twenty-four. But the governor also had advised me to be willing to change my plans if an unexpected opportunity came along. So I did. I would run for the legislature now.

I immediately called a friend in Beaumont who happened to be the sister of my brother's wife. We weren't related, but we were certainly close enough to share much respect and appreciation for each other. I told her my story and asked if I could get a teaching job in the South Park Independent School District. I had to support myself while I ran for office, and the Democratic primary in Texas was still months away. Luckily, there was an opening for a high-school physical science teacher, but school was beginning in two days and I was still in Washington, half a continent away. Nevertheless, I accepted the job and promised I would be there on time.

I left Washington that evening and drove all night and all the next day before having to stop for a rest. I got into Beaumont in time to take a shower and change clothes at my mother's house (I moved right back into the house where I had lived for my entire life) before rushing to the school in time to welcome my first class.

I had learned a lot from Jack Brooks and my summer on Capitol Hill, but that first political race would teach me twice as much about electoral campaigning—and hard-core politics—than I had ever thought possible.

When I started fund-raising, my first visit was to John Gray, a banker, family acquaintance, and later president of Lamar University. He gave me fifty dollars, a lot of money for a political donation then, and I thought I had arrived.

We bought one thousand posters with my campaign theme "Young, Responsive Leadership," the same theme I had used in high school and college. But the very same week we put out the signs, they were stolen. I was beside myself because those signs had represented my entire campaign fund.

Then I learned that high-school girls had taken the posters, apparently figuring that if they couldn't get posters of celebrities they would settle for mine. I found it hard to believe that the campaign signs with my picture on the upper two-thirds of the poster became sought after by young girls who wanted to put them up on their walls at home! I told myself, however, that the signs were in at least one thousand households and hopefully most of the houses contained several voters.

In those days, the Democratic primary was in May. The school year started in September, and teaching and campaigning for all the months in between wore me out. I never slept for more than a couple of hours at a time. The dual jobs were exhausting, physically and mentally.

THE DEATH OF WASHINGTON'S DEMOCRACY?

My sister, Mary Jo, was my campaign manager, and I don't know what I would have done without her and her organizational skills. With very little money, we made our own precinct voter lists and precinct maps and found ways to do other things we didn't think we could accomplish.

We developed a great army of kids from my classes as our "boots on the ground" and set out to knock on every door in Jefferson County. The voting age had not yet been lowered to eighteen—that wouldn't happen for another two years—so most high-school students weren't even old enough to vote for me. But over the course of three months or so, with the help of a lot of ninth and tenth graders, we went to sixty thousand homes with information about why I should be elected.

I had started teaching in Beaumont in 1969, fifteen years after the United States Supreme Court, in Brown v. Board of Education of Topeka, had ordered the public schools integrated. But segregation had not yet died in the South Park Independent School District.

I had been assigned to an almost new, all-white high school, some of whose students helped me organize the first Earth Day event in the state of Texas. That event and the political campaign I was waging for state representative were viewed as too activist by the principal. He set out to "punish" me by selecting me as one of the white teachers who would be transferred to an old, all-black high school.

The district's brain trust had decided to integrate the teaching staffs of the schools instead of the students. About 75 percent of the teaching staff of the black high school would be white, and about 75 percent of the staff of the white high school would be black.

The principal who chose me for transfer had no idea I was excited about the prospect of meeting and teaching a new population of students. I lived closer to Hebert, the black school, anyway.

The school district had allocated few resources for improvements at Hebert High. The school was famous for its great athletes, especially in football, but the physical education facility was a mess.

There weren't enough desks for the students in one of my physical science classes, and my biology students didn't have enough books or equipment to teach anything of significance. Ceilings leaked during rainstorms, and covered, outdoor walkways were full of rusted holes. The kids would step off the covered walk into the rain in order to avoid the cascades of water pouring through the holes. Even tugging on a classroom window covering could be a dangerous adventure. One day, a venetian blind broke during a class and hit me hard, cutting my face.

Hebert's principal, James Jackson, began to get a little frustrated with my constant demands for repairs. One day, when I asked why the school wouldn't fix an area outside my classroom that was flooded and wouldn't drain, he was furious. The district simply wasn't giving him the resources he needed. This time, though, he gave me permission to try to fix the problem. "You're so damn interested in it, Lampson, you take care of it," he said.

The flooded area had held water for so long that algal slime had developed, and it had become home for water bugs and mosquito larvae swimming all around.

I dispatched my biology students into the water to collect samples to analyze with the limited laboratory equipment that we had. They reluctantly gathered samples of water, vegetation, and mud. The students identified a three-quarter-inch water bug plus twenty-three other living organisms, including three suspected of being harmful to the human body.

Then we had to figure out what to do next. I gave the class a list of options, their chosen one being to take their findings to the

City of Beaumont Health Department. After verifying my students' research, the health department notified the school district that Hebert High School would not open the next day unless the health issues were corrected.

The students were elated that their work had closed the school, until they learned that the district had promptly dispatched workers to the campus. Within a few hours, the workers had fixed the problem by digging a small tunnel under the sidewalk and a shallow ditch to the street.

It was a simple, inexpensive fix for a health problem that, according to Mr. James Jackson, the principal, had plagued the school for twelve years. Repeated requests for help had simply been ignored.

District administrators, including Assistant Superintendent Paul Drawhorn, were furious with me over what they referred to as the "stunt," and for a while I thought I was going to be fired. But the principal was starting to like my willingness to go against the grain to get something done.

My students, meanwhile, had learned dual lessons. They had learned how to use the power of science and their biology lab tools to tell an environmental story. And our interaction with school administrators and city hall had taught them a great civics lesson about the power of engaged citizens in a democracy. Before then, nobody had ever asked, or cared about, what my students thought about anything. They felt empowered.

For me, the whole experience was a blast and whetted my appetite further for a larger niche in public service.

SIX

LEARNING FROM FAILURE AND SUCCESS

I was one of six candidates in that 1970 race for state representative and had been expected to finish last. I actually won the most votes in the May Democratic primary but fell short of the required 50 percent. So, I had to face a runoff against an attorney, Terry Doyle, from Port Arthur, the other major population center in the district.

Beaumont, which is in the northern part of Jefferson County, had a larger population than Port Arthur, so I expected to win the runoff and go to the legislature. There was no Republican candidate for the seat because Republicans still were scarce in Texas in those days. Instead, I learned my next political lessons—timing is everything, and as Election Day approaches, you turn out your own base—the hard way.

The runoff was held about a month later in June. The state representative race was the only race on the ballot, and there was little interest in the election. It was an awful time to try to get voters to the polls because most people were out of town or just too busy enjoying the first days of summer and the fact that their children were now out of school. And I topped off the problem with a major mistake.

I took Beaumont for granted and campaigned where I was least known, Port Arthur. Terry Doyle also campaigned in Port Arthur, his home base, and together we created a higher turnout of voters in Port Arthur than in the larger Beaumont, and Doyle won.

I should have campaigned where I was best known, Beaumont, and worked to turn out those votes. It was a hard lesson for a young, budding politician, but it would serve me well in future years. I did so poorly motivating the potential voters that even one of my main campaigners went fishing that day and failed to vote!

The students who campaigned for me learned as much that year about civics as they did physical science. One, Allan Ritter, was later elected to the Texas House of Representatives, and he told me he ran because of the experience he had helping me in that 1970 race.

Failure is the best and most consistent teacher, especially in science...and in politics.

One of the best things that happened to me during that campaign of 1970 was meeting the girl with whom I would spend the rest of my life. One day when I was campaigning in a shopping center in Beaumont, I remember holding a door open for a beautiful young lady and her mother. Not long after that incident I saw the same beautiful lady in the law office of a friend I was visiting and asked to be introduced. It was certainly unintentional, but it turns out that our first date in 1970 was to a political fundraiser for then Congressman Jack Brooks. Even though I was slow in the beginning of my pursuit of this beauty queen to be my wife, I never again had her out of my mind. Susan Floyd had graduated from Thomas Jefferson High School in Port Arthur, Texas, a competing school to my South Park High School in Beaumont. She had been crowned Miss Port Arthur in 1965 and competed in the Miss Texas pageant which she should have won. I guess there is politics in everything. I loved being with Susan and it was not long before we became inseparable. I could easily see the care and love she had for the people and things around her and I knew she was special. She has been a loving wife, an extraordinary mother to our two daughters, Hillary and Stephanie, the most fantastic and proud grandmother in the world, and a dedicated special education teacher who distinguished herself in life skills education to severely and profoundly challenged children. She has stood by me through all of my political adventures and sacrificed much to allow me to follow my dreams. Even though there have been difficult times through our life together, I can't imagine being without her and will always love her. Today she is as dedicated to the success of our grandchildren, who call her Marney, as she was to our children. We are blessed to have a close family and to have our children and grandchildren be the major part of our lives that they are.

Two years after my loss in the race for the Texas legislature, I was elected Jefferson County Democratic chairman. This was the year, 1972, that Democratic presidential nominee George McGovern would be trounced nationally and in Texas. My job was to go out and campaign for him and the other Democratic candidates in Jefferson County. And this was the first time I saw the real ugliness and downright hatred that can come out in politics.

The voters were very polarized. People either loved George McGovern or they hated him, and most Texans hated him. At times during that campaign, I was called some very ugly names, and on some occasions people even demanded that I leave public venues.

This was an early version of the modern wedge-issue campaign. The goal of our opponents seemed to be to trash McGovern and use his liberal views to taint him as much as possible and those who supported him in the same way. At times, it felt like people with pitchforks were coming after me , and I feared that the anger of some could turn physical. My chest often tightened, but I never backed down. Fortunately, all of the pummeling remained verbal. That campaign might have shown me a little of what was to come in future elections. I reminded myself, however, that when my brothers and sisters and I did harm to one another we always had the ability to forgive and forget. I was hoping that it would be the same way in politics.

I tried to stay positive, believing you catch more flies (and votes) with honey than with vinegar. The Democrats did OK in Jefferson County that year, but nationally and in Texas, McGovern was wiped out by Richard Nixon. And my process of learning through defeat was still not complete.

During the next election cycle, 1974, I lost a race for Jefferson County commissioner against a twenty-year incumbent. This loss was particularly painful because my margin of defeat in a Democratic runoff was only three-tenths of 1 percent. The lesson this time was how difficult it is to unseat an incumbent, long-time officeholder with high name identification.

* * * *

I was beginning to conclude that my role on this earth was not to be an elected public servant. So I dug in as a teacher, this time at Lamar University, where I taught real estate and business management for more than five years.

But I never quite abandoned my dreams and eventually was persuaded to run again, this time for Jefferson County tax assessor-collector. And, this time, I won!

The office included many administrative duties in addition to assessing and collecting property taxes on homes and businesses. It administered the voter registration system and handled automobile license renewals, among other duties.

But first and foremost, the office is identified with collecting taxes, a tricky political prospect at best. Americans of all stripes hate taxes. Our nation was forged in the hatred of taxes, and we haven't moved far from that original attitude.

But I moved quickly to develop a reputation for strong customer service, and I treated everyone fairly and equally. Not only was I collecting taxes, but I also was protecting the taxpayers' investment in their county government. And I ended up holding the office for almost two decades.

I regularly filed suit against homeowners who were delinquent in paying their taxes, and I also cracked down on large corporations, when necessary.

Once, an air carrier that operated between the Beaumont/ Port Arthur airport and the Austin airport owed Jefferson County more than $360,000 in back taxes. When I learned the company had enough cash in the bank to pay what was past due, I decided it was time to make a public example of a delinquent taxpayer. I went to court and obtained permission to seize one of the carrier's airliners. Then, accompanied by sheriff's deputies, I went to the airport to await an incoming flight. After the plane came to a stop on the tarmac, we took possession of it and told the company officials they could have it back when they paid their delinquent taxes.

My move was not without potentially negative political consequences because the passengers who were waiting to leave on that airplane were nearly all my constituents. They had been caught off guard and had their travel plans disrupted. But I think they understood. As taxpayers, they knew that they were better off if everyone paid their fair share of the community's tax burden. Besides, I could tell they were captivated by my boldness.

THE DEATH OF WASHINGTON'S DEMOCRACY?

The seizure paid off quickly when the carrier's representative showed up at my office the next morning with a check covering the taxes, penalty, interest, and costs. The company got its plane back, and our rate of collections soon became quite good. Other delinquents obviously had learned that it was in their best interest to pay their taxes.

Sometimes, however, being tough wasn't the right approach. I remember one woman who had been in default on the taxes on her home for many years. I worked with her in every way I could think of, even entering into multiple contracts for installment payments, to try to put off foreclosure. Finally, we ran out of options, and foreclosure became imminent. Then I learned this woman was an eighty-year-old widow who was dying of cancer. I wasn't about to throw her out on the streets.

So, in a panic, I spent the next two weeks looking for—and finally finding—a buyer for her house who would let her live there for the remainder of her life. I was successful in getting her delinquent taxes paid by the new owner, making the end of her life much more comfortable, and avoided creating a bad situation all the way around. Sometimes, vigorous enforcement of the law must be balanced with simple human respect and care.

I reorganized and modernized the tax office and cut the cost of collecting taxes in Jefferson County from $4 million per year to about $1 million per year.

The tax office was where I really cut my political teeth. It was where I came to understand that people will support you when they believe you care about them. Beginning with the tax office and throughout my public career, I always tried to instill in those who worked with me one basic premise: always be responsive to the public in any request that comes our way.

Even if it was a complaint about a pothole that needed fixing, for which the tax office had no responsibility, staffers were instructed to stay on the phone until they found someone who could solve the "customer's" problem and then tell them that if they ever needed anything else to give us a call and we would always try to be helpful. As in retail sales, the customer is always right.

People will remember individual public servants favorably if they had a positive experience dealing with them or their staff. People soon learned that they could come to me for just about anything and find help with difficult problems. The word-of-mouth about my responsiveness and efficiency was more valuable than a million-dollar TV ad buy.

My constituents' satisfaction with my customer service and their trust in my tax-collecting judgment ultimately would reward me with my first term in the U.S. House of Representatives.

SEVEN

TORCHING THE HOUSE

In August 1814, during the War of 1812, British troops invaded Washington, DC, and marched into the still-unfinished Capitol building. They gathered rowdily in the old House Chamber (now Statuary Hall), where, according to some historical reports, they were addressed by their commander.

"The question before the House today is should this bastion of democracy continue to stand," he said, standing upon the Speaker's chair.

"No!" his soldiers shouted in unison, setting the building afire.

The Capitol was heavily damaged, but Providence smiled upon the new nation when a long rain put out the British fires before they could destroy the building.

Nearly two hundred years later, the same Capitol—or at least the House of Representatives—was to be torched again, this time in a figurative sense, and the nation still hasn't recovered.

The perpetrators of the new attack weren't foreign troops or foreign terrorists, but a group of Republican congressmen intent on reversing long-time Democratic control of the House by "burning down" the institution.

That was the quoted goal of their leader, Newt Gingrich, a backbench congressman from Georgia, who had schemed for years about how to attain it.

His theory—"We must burn this village in order to save it"— had not too many years earlier been left in the jungles of Vietnam as a remarkably failed strategy. But Gingrich was resurrecting it in terms of political warfare.

The plan was so audacious and far-fetched that few people thought it could work, and even fewer people thought the American public could be hoodwinked so profoundly. But Gingrich's scheme, which introduced the country to the "politics of personal destruction," was to be extraordinarily successful.

In May 1988, Gingrich persuaded seventy-seven other Republican House members, including Tom DeLay of Texas, to join him in bringing ethics charges against Democratic House Speaker Jim Wright, who also was from Texas. They alleged that the speaker had used a book he had written to raise political funds for himself while circumventing campaign finance laws and House ethics rules.

It was true that Speaker Wright had written a book and that Democratic interest groups had frequently bought copies in bulk. Those facts and all the fiction that Gingrich, DeLay, and company could muster finally convinced Common Cause—the "good government" lobby—into agreeing that the matter should at least be investigated.

The politically driven investigation became a circus. The House Ethics Committee was forced into conducting a full proctology examination of everything Speaker Wright had ever done, while the full-throated chattering of his detractors filled the broadcast airways. The work of the "People's House" was sullied, then stymied.

Jim Wright, one of the toughest, but most practical, men ever to lead the U.S. House of Representatives, suddenly had to decide how to deal with the new politics of personal destruction. He resigned both the speakership and his House seat from Fort Worth, falling on his sword in the hope of restoring public confidence in the institution he loved.

Both Texas and the country lost a lot from that decision because Jim Wright was an extraordinary thinker and problem solver.

Years earlier, when he was mayor of Fort Worth, his office once got almost simultaneous phone calls, one complaining about swarms of blackbirds in a neighborhood and the other complaining of a young boy shooting a BB gun. The mayor got in his car, picked up the young man with the air rifle, took him to the neighborhood with the blackbird invasion, and both problems were addressed. That was Speaker Wright's approach to problems at the national level as well.

When Jim Wright was Speaker and for many years before that, the U.S. House of Representatives was a congenial place to work. Lawmakers regularly had differences of opinion over issues and how best to govern the country. And they would spend long hours debating their differences, often heatedly, in the House chamber and in committee rooms. But with rare exceptions, they were civil to one another. After the workday ended, Democrats and Republicans ate together and socialized together. Over dinner or cocktails or at the golf course, they often found workable compromises on difficult issues. That's how Washington is supposed to work. And this partisanship with civility was still being practiced during the administration of the first President Bush (1989–1993).

When the Democrats who ran the House in those days wanted to make a political issue of something that President George H. W. Bush opposed, they included the provision in a bill they knew he would veto. After the veto, the Democratic majority would agree to resend the same bill to the president, but without the provision or language the president opposed, and he would sign it.

Everybody made his political points. Democrats in Congress would get credit for helping to pass a bill addressing an important issue, be it cleaner air or international trade. And Republicans could tell their supporters that they had been able to remove some objectionable language through a presidential veto.

More importantly, Congress and the president had addressed the people's business instead of letting important legislation be held hostage—as is usually the case today—to hyperpartisan debate between Democrats and Republicans on Capitol Hill and their surrogate talking heads on cable TV.

Remember how important President Barack Obama's health-care reform initiative was to millions of Americans? Remember how long it took Congress to pass it? It took more than a year, and only after a superhuman effort by the president and the Democratic congressional leadership. Not one single Republican in the House or the Senate voted for the bill. Thankfully, the Democrats had regained control of Capitol Hill by then. But the setting aside of partisan differences for the good of the country, which had helped President Johnson win landmark civil rights legislation less than fifty years earlier, hadn't been rediscovered.

The beginning of that congressional breakdown can be traced directly to the scorched-earth, win-at-any-cost partisanship that Newt Gingrich, Tom DeLay, and their cohorts began practicing in the late 1980s.

By 1989, after House Minority Whip Dick Cheney was appointed secretary of defense by the first President Bush, the House Republican caucus selected Gingrich to succeed him. Democrats were still in the House majority, but Gingrich was being rewarded for his successful, malicious campaign against Jim Wright.

Gingrich's new position in the Republican caucus was entirely to formalize the Gingrich-DeLay belief that if Republicans ever were to gain the House majority, they first would have to blow up the institution and then rebuild it from the rubble.

THE DEATH OF WASHINGTON'S DEMOCRACY?

Gingrich, DeLay, and their minions in the House, especially the newly minted "Gang of Seven"—seven freshmen who made hours of floor speeches every day—railed against anything and everything that could remotely be exaggerated into ethical lapses in the House, which had been under the control of Democrats for almost forty years.

The Gingrich-DeLay crowd even started comparing themselves to Moses and God's "chosen people," who, according to the Bible, spent forty years wandering around the wilderness before finding their way into the promised land.

The Republicans' tactics and message were entirely about assigning "good" and "evil" tags to the Republican and Democratic parties, respectively, writing what would become the instruction manual for Republican election campaigns for at least the next two decades.

No party is entitled to a mortal lock on either house of Congress or the presidency. Just because the Democrats had controlled the U.S. House for so long was no reason to assume that should continue.

But our elections are the appropriate instruments of change in our government institutions, not gerrymandered redistricting plans (which I will discuss shortly) or the misuse of religion. It is repugnant to spin elections around who is allegedly "good" and who is "evil." No politician should ever misuse religious language in the pursuit of public policy or electoral gains – something that Republicans have done for the past twenty years.

Elections and campaigns are supposed to be about issues and solutions, not which church an officeholder or candidate attends— or doesn't attend.

NICK LAMPSON

* * * *

Democrats still controlled Congress in 1991, despite the destructive politics of Gingrich and DeLay, and I was still the Jefferson County tax assessor-collector. Democrats also were still in control in Austin, where the Texas Legislature was faced with the task of redrawing boundary lines for Texas's congressional districts to accommodate the population changes reflected in the 1990 census. At that time, redistricting was still a once-in-a-decade chore. To be sure, some redistricting actions, even though starting immediately after the census, carried into the decade due to court consideration and actions. But redistricting wars still always began immediately following the completion of each decadal census.

Thanks to a strong increase in population, as counted in the 1990 census, Texas was awarded three new congressional districts to bring the state's total to thirty. With Democratic governor Ann Richards's approval, the legislature approved a new map that largely retained the status quo for the twenty-seven incumbent U.S. House members from Texas. All twenty-seven, nineteen Democrats and eight Republicans, would be reelected in 1992. The three new congressional districts would be won by Democrats to give Democrats twenty-two congressional seats from Texas.

If Governor Richards and the Democratic legislative majority had wanted to declare open partisan warfare, they would have drastically redrawn the congressional map to break up blocs of Republican votes around the state and attach them to solidly Democratic districts.

But that was not what redistricting was about, at least not yet. Redistricting was intended to make once-in-a-decade adjustments in congressional district boundaries based on population changes, while ensuring that "communities of interest" remained intact.

THE DEATH OF WASHINGTON'S DEMOCRACY?

Although not defined literally by law, a "community of interest" is generally a group of people united by shared interests or values. These interests could include common history or culture, a common racial or ethnic background, or a variety of economic or other ties that create a community of voters who share distinct interests.

All that would change in 2003, when Texas's Republican leaders would make partisanship the overriding "community of interest" for drastically redrawing congressional districts between censuses—much to the confusion of Texas voters.

* * * *

In 1994, voters around the nation elected Republicans over Democrats in numbers large enough to give Republicans control of the House of Representatives. Even Jack Brooks, my old Capitol Hill boss and teacher, saw his forty-two-year congressional career come to an end in the so-called "Republican Revolution." He was unseated by Steve Stockman, an ultraconservative political novice, partly because Brooks's district, redrawn in 1991, had become slightly less Democratic and partly because he had angered conservatives earlier that year by supporting legislation to ban access to assault weapons.

Riding the crest of the Republican tide, Newt Gingrich, the new House speaker, and his lieutenant, Tom DeLay, colluded to become even better at the politics of personal destruction, mainly because their new House majority was very thin. Republicans had a House majority of twenty-six votes by 1996, the high point of their numerical strength. That meant Democrats only had to reclaim a net fourteen districts to regain the majority. By 2001, the GOP majority had narrowed to nine votes, meaning that all the Democrats needed then was a five-seat swing to be back in charge. Republican leaders were very much in fear of losing the majority they had so recently won.

As early as 1996, DeLay, then the House majority whip, had begun to assure his Republican colleagues that their party would pick up another four to six House seats from Texas by 2002. Packing committed Republican voters into reconfigured congressional districts would cost some incumbent Democrats their seats, and the newly elected Republicans might be enough to keep the GOP in control of the House.

Texas had been trending Republican since George W. Bush defeated Ann Richards as governor in 1994, and DeLay refused to believe that Texans would want to continue electing both Democrats and Republicans to represent them.

It was among a ton of things he would be wrong about, but that wouldn't stop him from scorching the political interests of millions of Texas voters.

EIGHT

CONGRESSMAN LAMPSON

After nearly two decades of public service at the county level, I decided to run for the U.S. House in 1996. I was ready to test my talents on the national stage, to return to the Capitol Hill campus I had loved and learned from that long-ago summer during my college days.

I would run against Steve Stockman for the seat he had wrested from my mentor, Jack Brooks, during the previous election cycle. My decision actually had been made on the night of the 1994 election, when Stockman hung up the phone on Brooks during Brooks's call to congratulate Stockman on his win. I remember the evening well. It was the conclusion of a very long and hard day of campaigning after weeks of preparation. That election was no different from many, many others preceding it, except that the mood of the electorate was beginning to change. In this particular campaign the issue many people had been talking about was the Brady gun-control bill. It had been passed earlier that year by the Democratic caucus in response to the shooting of President Ronald Reagan. Jack Brooks had voted for that legislation, and while it did not appear to be the only reason people were organizing against his reelection, it became the most talked-about issue affecting his continued service in the U.S. House of Representatives. Many people later talked about their disappointment in his loss. Some who voted against him said they really didn't want to see him out of office; they just wanted to send a message to him that he should pay more attention to his constituents. Regardless of the reason, 1994 became a sweep of Republicans into office across the United States, giving control of the House of Representatives to the Republicans for the first time in almost forty years.

As that election drew to a close and Jack Brooks realized he would not win reelection, his chief of staff, Sharon Matts, dialed the cell-phone number of Steve Stockman to congratulate him on his victory. I was standing nearby Congressman Brooks and Miss Matts as she dialed the phone in the front of a television camera. She spoke to newly elected Steve Stockman and turned to hand the phone to Congressman Brooks for him to offer his words of concession. Stockman abruptly disconnected the telephone call. A stunned and confused Jack Brooks held the phone as he heard Stockman hang up on him, and he turned to the people around him and commented, "You got what you voted for." It was clearly a statement of disappointment and wonderment at the person who was being allowed to step into the position he had held and worked so hard at for so many years to address the needs of a struggling but growing community. The outcome of that election left us confused and disappointed.

My decision to run for Congress was made that night. I was encouraged by, among others, my friend Don Stephens, who had worked for Brooks for many years and had been a political science professor at Lamar University when I was a student.

But it wouldn't be easy.

Texas Republicans, unhappy with the redistricting plan approved by the legislature in 1991, had filed a "reverse discrimination" lawsuit, claiming that it violated recent U.S. Supreme Court decisions by carving out new congressional districts dominated by Hispanic and African American voters. Those were the three new districts added after the 1990 census.

THE DEATH OF WASHINGTON'S DEMOCRACY?

In 1996, a three-judge federal court eventually upheld most of the legislative plan but changed the boundaries of the three new districts and several districts adjoining them, including the one in which I was running. In all, thirteen of the state's thirty districts were affected.

In that same year and with a great deal of hard work, I won a crowded Democratic primary without a runoff. But the federal court, which had only minimally changed the boundaries of my district, threw out the primary results and ordered a special election for the congressional seat to be held on the same day as the general election in November. That meant the voters would have to vote on two ballots on the same day at the same voting location. One ballot would be for the general election, and the other would be for the special election for the congressional seat I was seeking. To make matters worse, any number of Democrats and Republicans could run in the special congressional race. It was referred to as an open primary and meant that anyone could file and seek that office at that time. I am still convinced the court, dominated by a majority of Republican appointees, had ordered the special election to give an advantage to Stockman, the Republican incumbent.

Additionally, Stockman tried to pull two dirty tricks of his own to improve his chances and keep me from winning.

First, he shopped around until he found someone allegedly named "Jack Brooks" to also get into the race. The idea was to use this familiar Democratic name to siphon Democratic votes from me. The Jack Brooks name was so well-known that Stockman believed people would vote for Brooks by accident, thinking it was the same one who had served for so many years. This could give Stockman the advantage he needed to win. This "Jack Brooks," however, was not the former congressman who had represented the

60

district for forty-two years. In fact, he didn't even live anywhere near the district. He lived more than three hundred miles away in Uvalde, west of San Antonio. A congressional candidate doesn't have to live in the district. But he has to use a name on the ballot by which he has been "commonly known" for at least two years prior to the election.

When I learned that this Mr. Brooks had not always gone by Jack, I challenged him in court. I also encouraged a television station to interview Brooks's wife at their Uvalde home. The cameraman and reporter traveled across Texas from Beaumont to Uvalde where they interviewed Mrs. Brooks. When the taped interview was played in court, and the judge heard Mrs. Brooks refer to her husband as Gary, the judge laughed out loud and ruled in my favor. Now that Gary Brooks had to use his real name on the ballot, he dropped out of the race, and I had successfully cleared one hurdle.

The next hurdle erected by Mr. Stockman and his cronies came in the form of Geraldine Sam, an African American teacher from La Marque. She had lost to me in the regular (and later invalidated) Democratic primary but was recruited to run against me again in that special open election. It was rumored that Vic Rogers of Beaumont, a substantial Republican benefactor and supporter of Stockman, was bankrolling a lot of Sam's campaign, including providing her with a car. The goal was to dilute the strongly Democratic African American vote, which I was expected to win. Republicans hoped Mrs. Sam would take enough Democratic votes from me to enable Stockman to win the special election outright with a majority and avoid a runoff.

But Stockman got only 46 percent of the vote, I got 44 percent, and Mrs. Sam managed only 10 percent. Since no one got a majority, Stockman and I prepared for a runoff set for December 15, only ten days before Christmas, when most people would be busy preparing for the holidays, not relishing the idea of going to the polls again.

Stockman's Republican supporters, including Tom DeLay, believed there would be a very low turnout for the runoff, which would benefit the incumbent. But I worked hard, and with a great organization and lots of help from good friends, we produced a high voter turnout, enough for me to beat Stockman with more than 52 percent of the vote.

An enormous contributor to my victory was the Democratic Congressional Campaign Committee (DCCC), chaired by my fellow Texan, Martin Frost of Dallas. The DCCC helped me with issues, advocacy, fund-raising, and more.

Martin Frost was an unsung hero in Texas campaigns in the 1990s. He recruited candidates who could appeal across party lines and counseled us when our campaigns had bad days. Most importantly, he directed money and independent resources to help our campaigns compete in the critical last month before an election.

Fund-raising is a tough act for anybody, even for somebody who had been in politics for as long as I had been. On my first trip to Washington, DC, after that election, I met with some of the outgoing staffers of the Democratic Congressional Campaign Committee. They tried to talk me out of running but ended up telling me that if I wanted to win I would have to raise significant amounts of money, something in the range of $850,000. That really seemed to be too much of a goal for me to achieve. Remember the story I told earlier about what I was told were the ten most important things to focus on in a campaign? That's right, each of the ten was the same: "raise money." This was when I first received that advice. I was clearly getting the picture that fund-raising was the most important job in running for Congress.

When I returned to Beaumont, my campaign manager, Jacquelyn Davis, and I hired a fund-raiser. Her name was Jacqui Osman and, like most of my campaign staffers, was young and inexperienced but had a mountain of enthusiasm. They kept me in a room with a locked door so that I would not be disturbed, and made me raise money. That's all I did—dial the phone all day long and ask people to make contributions to my campaign for Congress. By the end of that grueling affair, including my days upon days of dialing for dollars, I had spent $1.7 million and had only a $60,000 debt, which was paid off in the first month of my service as a newly elected member of Congress. I had raised twice the amount I said earlier that I could not raise. I truly wanted to be the congressman from the Ninth Congressional District of Texas. Money came from people all over the United States almost faster than we could keep up with. This race was popular and reached a national audience. I remember a contribution of seven one-dollar bills coming in the mail from an elderly lady in Pennsylvania and a concert performed in Houston by Don Henley of the Eagles at which we raised over $150,000. It was as exciting as anything I could remember doing.

While I was still serving my community as the Jefferson County tax assessor-collector, I had started the Italian American Society of Beaumont, and that group became an extraordinary resource for fund-raising. I loved my Italian heritage. When I began running for Congress, I had to reach into other communities. Galveston was going to be very key, and I knew an important businessman named Vic Fertitta lived there and owned a hotel on the Galveston Seawall. I immediately reached out to him but was unsuccessful in securing the meeting I sought. After many unanswered phone calls, I sent a letter to him and mentioned his cousin in Beaumont. He took my next phone call and asked how I knew his cousin. When I told him he was a member of the Italian American organization I had founded, he paused and said, "Are you Italian?" When I responded yes, he immediately invited me over to have lunch with him. He became of significant help to me in winning that race for Congress. Later, his son, Tilman Fertitta, who is the founder of Landry Restaurants and has become a TV personality, also was beneficial in helping me get the resources necessary to put me in the U.S. Congress. I will always be grateful for their friendship.

Although raising money for political campaigns is a much-maligned enterprise, money is an indicator of a serious candidate—or a lightweight. Money can't assure an election outcome, but it can even the playing field.

Martin Frost wanted to illustrate that when the playing field in Texas was level, Democrats held their own and won races. We both held a solid belief that our ideas were better—and helped more people—than the Republicans' ideas.

Our theory was that independent-thinking, middle-class families, in Texas and elsewhere, would respond to the Democratic arguments on economic issues more favorably than to the hot-button "cultural" concerns that traditionally motivated religious conservatives.

And, in my first congressional election, Texans understood that Republicans did not have an exclusive hold on the Lord God Almighty. I was fully engaged with people of faith in my district, as I had always been in my public service, and I made sure that Republicans did not succeed in casting the election in terms of good and evil.

My 1996 election was an early win for Democrats who were finding new and better ways to reach out to voters, telling them the truth just as loudly as the other side was trying to drown out the truth.

Late that election night, President Bill Clinton called to tell me that he and Hillary "were dancing in the White House over my victory." I was on my way to Congress, but only after a tough battle. And little did I know then that this battle had been just a precursor of what my future would hold in the game of politics.

* * * *

Historically, the U.S. government has thrived on partisanship. The Great Compromise at the birth of this nation was to bring many voices together. Our strength was in our differences, our diversity of opinions and ideas. From that strength, we forged solutions to our challenges and met our ever-changing needs.

As mentioned before, George Washington cautioned us in his farewell address as the first president of the United States not to allow parties to gain prominence in relation to the strength of our Congress. He feared and warned us that the desire for partisan unity would overshadow the unity of Congress and adversely affect its ability to function. The party could become more important than Congress itself.

The key was an ability and willingness to compromise. Partisans debated and pressed for their respective viewpoints, but in the end they sought common ground for the good of the country. That was one of the most important lessons I had learned as a young congressional intern in Washington in 1969.

To my great disappointment, Capitol Hill was an altogether different place when I returned in January 1997 to take my seat in the U.S. House of Representatives. Partisanship had taken steroids, replacing compromise with a buzz saw that chewed up civility, respect, and effective governance. Lawmakers from opposing parties were loathe to seek common ground, or, in many cases, to even talk with one another.

Rather than many voices coming together, partisans were listening only to those who agreed with them. The House that Gingrich and DeLay had burned down was barely functioning. The few of us who tried to stand in the middle and build consensus were in constant danger of being pummeled from both sides.

So, as I had since my early days as tax assessor-collector, I concentrated primarily on constituent services. "Work hard, do more, and do it better," I told myself and my staff. If, in the end, my only legacy would be that I was a tireless public servant, it would be a worthy legacy.

I taught my staff how to solve people's problems just as I had done in the tax office years earlier. Today, instead of potholes, it was tracking down a missing Social Security check for a senior citizen or helping a disabled veteran find a contact at the Veterans Administration. Problems were like puzzles, and I loved to master them. I often felt like a social worker, and once I was even recognized by an association of social workers for my work on behalf of constituents in Southeast Texas. A Houston Chronicle survey, published in 2002, showed that my congressional operation handled more constituent cases than any other representative's office from the greater Houston area.[8]

I also was the ranking member on the House Space and Aeronautics Subcommittee. As such, I worked hard for more resources for the country's space program, including the Johnson Space Center, a huge job creator in my district, which was centered around Beaumont, my home, and included Galveston and parts of Harris County, as well.

8   Karen Masterson, "District 18 may pay price for Jackson Lee's pace," *The Houston Chronicle*, September 1, 2002.

I loved my involvement with the Science, Space and Technology Committee. The members of that committee were allowed to envision the future as we listened to the dreams and works of scientists from all disciplines. It provided the opportunity to interact with risk-taking astronauts, brilliant and dedicated scientists and futurists. So, when my friend George Abbey, director of the Johnson Space Center, asked me through Israel Galvan, our friend in common, to meet with me and a group of five scientists from five different nations, I jumped at the opportunity. The scientists were flying to the United States to meet privately with me in a hotel across the street from the Johnson Space Center. The scientists, all particle physicists, were from the United States, Germany, Spain, and Italy. The lead scientist, I learned, was Dr. Sam Ting, who did particle physics research at the Massachusetts Institute of Technology. They proceeded to tell me about a project called the Alpha Magnetic Spectrometer, AMS for short. The AMS was a project intended to be comparable in the scientific world to a Superconducting Super Collider like the Large Hadron Collider (LHC) in Geneva, Switzerland. The LHC is the world's largest and most powerful particle accelerator. The LHC is an extremely complex system of tubes, lights, electricity, magnets, and much more extending in a circle for twenty-six miles. My simple explanation of its purpose is to study the particles remaining after collisions of atoms in an effort to determine their effect on the human body. This is information we must have to protect our astronauts during deep space travel and will provide many more benefits here on Earth pertaining to human health. Neither then, nor now, do I understand particle physics, but Dr. Ting began to explain this project he had conceived of many years earlier.

Dr. Ting had gathered a group of sixty scientists from the sixteen nations participating in the International Space Station to finance and build this AMS project. Dr. Ting explained that the United States had promised as its part to finance the transportation of the AMS aboard the U.S. space shuttle and install the AMS on the International Space Station. During his two-hour explanation, he told me that the project was near completion and the partners in this international project had been told by the U.S. government that it would not honor its commitment. President Bush's science adviser, John Marburger, was not confident this was necessary science and, therefore, opposed the project; and the president had made the decision to end the era of operating space shuttles. Dr. Ting explained this was a devastating blow to the international collaboration that had been operating among scientist friends for many years, and they had already spent a great deal of money. He asked me if I would champion this project and attempt to reverse the actions of the U.S. government. I felt overwhelmed but honored that he would think I had the ability to be helpful in this significant need that would impact both international relations and the future of a major science project. Certainly, I would do what I could.

I believed that the AMS was a worthwhile project, that not allowing the project to reach its ultimate destination would have been harmful to future scientific discovery and progress, and that it was important to fulfill our commitment. Neglecting to do so would let down our international partners, sour important relationships, and damage our credibility, not to mention waste a significant number of taxpayer dollars. The additional shuttle-flight cost would be marginal compared to the work and money that had already gone into the project. I brought in my Science Committee staffer, Carrie Chess, who was completing her master's degree in space policy at George Washington University and, together with Senator Kay Bailey Hutchison (R-TX), we got to work.

I arranged meetings with NASA administrator Michael Griffin, wrote letters to President George Bush, and met with his representatives at the Office of Management and Budget. I lobbied my colleagues, including those in other NASA districts, the leadership of key congressional committees, and House leadership. The real hurdles were securing additional funding and getting everyone on board with the idea of possibly flying past the arbitrary cut-off date of 2010 for ending space shuttle flights.

I sponsored an amendment to the NASA Authorization Act, which passed in October 2008. The language I had inserted into the bill follows:

(5) For Space Operations, $6,074,700,000, of which—

1. $150,000,000 Shall be for an additional space shuttle flight to deliver the Alpha Magnetic Spectrometer to the International Space Station;
2. Additional flight to deliver the Alpha Magnetic Spectrometer and other scientific equipment and payloads to the International Space Station;
3. In general in addition to the flying of the baseline manifest as described in subsection D, the administrator shall take all necessary steps to fly one additional Space Shuttle flight to deliver the Alpha Magnetic Spectrometer and other scientific equipment and payloads to the International Space Station prior to the retirement of the Space Shuttle. The purpose of the mission required to be planned under this subsection shall be to ensure the active use of the United States portion of the International Space Station as a National Laboratory by the delivery of the Alpha Magnetic Spectrometer, and to the extent practical, the delivery of flight ready research experiments.

The AMS was taken to the ISS by astronaut Mark Kelly in 2010. Data has been streaming back to Earth for study by Dr. Ting and his team of now almost five hundred scientists. I was out of Congress by then, having been defeated due to the effects of redistricting in Texas. Had I been successful in that reelection, I would have become chairman of the Space and Aeronautics Subcommittee and would have been able to provide an even greater service to our nation regarding NASA advancements. Interestingly, the person who became chairman of that subcommittee was Congresswoman Gabrielle Giffords from Arizona, who was shot in the head in an attempted assassination not many months later. She is the wife of astronaut Mark Kelly, who commanded the special shuttle flight carrying the AMS to the ISS. When I think back on that reelection season, I never understood why people in the Johnson Space Center area chose to vote against their interests and against me for the sole purpose of my having a D after my name on the ballot instead of an R. Labels are a huge detriment to the potential good works of our government.

* * * *

In a limited but important way, I also was able to champion the cause of bipartisanship. Unfortunately, the effort was sparked by a tragedy in my district.

About three months after I took my first congressional oath, a twelve-year-old girl from Friendswood was abducted and found murdered two weeks later. I felt compelled to try to prevent a similar tragedy from happening to another family.

This led to my founding a few months later of the Congressional Caucus on Missing and Exploited Children to address the problem in a coordinated way and to increase awareness of child safety in our communities, particularly among families, schools, and law-enforcement officers. This caucus grew into the largest bipartisan, issue-oriented caucus in the House.

With the caucus pursuing nonpartisan objectives, we saw one another as part of a team working for the American people, as if we were family members working for the good of the larger family, not a group working for a particular political party. Some of our other colleagues in Congress also began to see the value of bipartisan work, but uncompromising partisanship remained dominant on Capitol Hill.

The caucus was directly responsible for nationalizing the successful Amber Alert system, which notifies the public of missing children, and it became a forum for us to weigh in on other legislation to help families protect their children.

We also sponsored legislation to fund law-enforcement efforts against child pornography and exploitation on the Internet. And, locally, the caucus helped launch Project Safe Place in Harris and Galveston counties, a project bringing businesses together to aid children who are in trouble and need a safe place to go. John Walsh, host of the TV show America's Most Wanted, and the National Center for Missing and Exploited Children recognized me for my work to protect kids.

* * * *

I was fortunate to get to know Representative Doug Bereuter, a Republican from Montana, when I first arrived in Congress, and he invited me to participate in the NATO Parliamentary Assembly. I didn't accept his invitation during my first term, but I did attend the international meetings of that group during the next six years. They were great—and humbling—learning experiences for me and provided important opportunities to represent the United States' interests abroad.

The NATO Parliamentary Assembly is an organization of representatives of parliaments from each of the NATO nations. There are typically two meetings during each year; the first meeting is at the NATO headquarters in Brussels, Belgium, while the second meeting is held in one of the NATO nation states. The assembly would discuss issues of importance to the alliance. One such issue, for example, was the expansion of NATO. I had the pleasure of serving during the time when NATO membership was expanded to include all of the Balkan states following the dissolution of the USSR. As Russia began to be aggressive in its attempt to expand its borders and include those several nations, they sought assistance by reaching out to NATO for their inclusion and protection. In order for NATO to accept that expanded membership, the nations had to prove their military capabilities, prowess, and financial ability to support all of the allies associating together in NATO. It was my honor to serve as a delegate during the time when the NATO Parliamentary Assembly had to determine eligibility one country at a time. Traveling to each of the countries and observing the lengths to which each nation went in preparation to show off their capabilities was a huge education for me. The esteem in which they held NATO, and particularly the United States of America, made me quite proud of my homeland and the good work we have done to promote peace around the world.

I remember a meeting with representatives of the Organization for Economic and Cooperative Development in Paris around the year 2000 that was of particular importance to the American airline industry and the flying public. The new European Union was trying to stop commercial airliners from the United States from landing at airports in Europe if they had been retrofitted with "hush kits," devices designed to lessen engine noise. Even with the special devices, the Europeans said, the planes were still too noisy. They wanted the Americans to fly only planes with new engines, which was an obvious effort to promote European airplanes and restrict the use of ours.

While arguing that point, I caught myself and thought, "Wow, what is this kid from South Park High School in Beaumont, Texas, doing in Paris, France, representing the whole United States of America?" What an awesome feeling! I could have only dreamed of doing such a thing. Yet, there I was, sitting among representatives of countries from all over Europe, and they were listening to me. I will never forget that moment.

We Americans eventually won the issue, allowing our airliners equipped with hush kits to continue flying into airports in Europe.

I loved those meetings and the opportunity to get to know people from other parts of the world. I realized how important it was for the United States to have its public servants, such as myself, go to other countries and speak out for America. Congressional travel is important for many reasons. We were and are great ambassadors for growing business and tourism, as well as promoting the safety of our country. More people should understand this and not criticize the trips members of Congress make.

Just as family vacations bring families closer together, spending time with work colleagues allows each person to get to know the other better. Travel provides magnificent opportunities to learn more about the world in which we live, our global neighbors, and how others govern themselves in other cultures. I never failed to return home without knowledge beneficial to my constituents, making that travel worth far more than the cost of the trip.

THE DEATH OF WASHINGTON'S DEMOCRACY?

* * * *

I was in Congress for most of the second President Bush's administration, and I still find his bizarre economic policy insidious, which built up a deficit so overwhelming that it represents a tax on my grandchildren and who knows how many other future generations. I voted to reduce our nation's debt and deficits, but my opinion, shared by many of my colleagues, was stifled by the congressional majority and the White House.

Not only did the second Bush administration defer payment on the nation's bills, it also was dishonest about the cost of those bills. Every year, for example, the wars in Afghanistan and Iraq were designated by the White House, for budgetary purposes, as "unanticipated emergencies." The bills for those wars have come due, and we Americans will be shocked at the ultimate cost. Our losses in human treasure already have been too much to bear.

I voted with the majority for the Iraq war. I was really conflicted, but at the end I stood on the House floor and said publicly that I must make a decision. I chose to trust the president for the information, including Iraq's alleged but nonexistent weapons of mass destruction that his administration was putting out to the country and to Congress, on which my vote was based.

Today I feel betrayed because whether the president knew the truth or not, people around him had to have had better information than what they were sharing with us in Congress and with the American people. We, as a people, must find ways to restore the credibility of the presidency and to regain confidence that our leader is giving us the best possible information and that Congress is truly acting in the best long-term interests of our nation. It was in that vein that I said what I said and voted in the manner in which I did.

Meanwhile, other policies of President George W. Bush and Republicans in Congress allowed the financial industry to run itself into the ground with greed, costing Americans from all walks of life untold billions in lost savings and pensions, and costing millions of people their jobs.

The Wall Street bailouts, initiated by Bush and completed under President Obama, will add still another $2 trillion—or more—to the costs of Bush's wildly failed budget and economic policy.

NINE

TOM DeLAY, THE HOUSE BULLY

Before he became a politician, Tom DeLay was a pest exterminator—no joke—in Sugar Land in Southeast Texas. In 1978, he was elected to the Texas House of Representatives, where his six-year career can best be summed up in one word: unremarkable.

He received little media attention, had little impact on the legislative process, was disliked by many of his colleagues, and played more than he worked. In his own book, he admits to the nickname "Hot Tub Tom," given for his extracurricular activities in Austin.

How this same man ended up, not too many years later, as the majority leader of the U.S. House of Representatives is an indictment of the American political system, a graphic illustration of how money, greed, and ambition can hijack the legislative process.

In Washington, DeLay, as opposed to his hot-tubbing alter ego in Austin, would soon prove to be surprisingly effective in raising money for himself and other Republican candidates, delivering votes, and generally being a pain in the behind to Democrats on the other side of the aisle.

His methods were less than admirable—and, in some cases, less than ethical.

The New York Times reported on October 12, 1986, in an article about six newly elected Republican congressman and their effect on the politics of the state of Texas. The group was termed "the Texas Six-Pack" and included Dick Armey, Mac Sweeney,

Larry Combest, Beau Boulter, Joe Barton, and Tom DeLay. The Texas Six-Pack built their strength on the basis of Ronald Reagan's earlier win of the presidency and began to usher into Texas politics a new kind of campaign; the article reported that "theirs is a campaign whose hallmark is negativism, pessimism, and cynicism."[9] It foretold of what was likely to come for Texas and the United States in a new world of politics.

DeLay began his rise in the House's Republican ranks in 1988, when he was appointed deputy whip by then minority whip Dick Cheney. When the Republicans gained control of the House in 1995, following the 1994 elections, DeLay was elected majority whip against the wishes of Republican House Speaker-elect Newt Gingrich of Georgia.

DeLay had been an early ally in Gingrich's successful scorched-earth campaign to wrest control of the House from Democrats, including the successful effort to force Democratic Speaker Jim Wright from Congress in 1988.

But DeLay was not always on good terms with Gingrich or with Dick Armey, the Texas Republican Six-Pack running mate and the House majority leader from 1995 to 2003. DeLay reportedly considered them uncommitted to "Christian" values—whatever that meant to Republican insiders.

Hot Tub Tom was now differentiating between "good" and "evil" political figures, and he would soon turn on Gingrich, his former friend.

In the GOP heyday of the 104th Congress (1995–1997), DeLay described the Republican leadership as a triumvirate of Gingrich,

---

9   James C. McKinley, Jr. "DeLay is Convicted in Texas Donation Case," New York Times, Nov. 24, 2010, http//www.nytimes.com/2010/11/25/us/politics/25delay.html.

Armey, and himself. Robert Dreyfuss, who wrote for the Texas Observer, said of Tom DeLay that "according to both his friends and foes in Washington, DeLay was the single most powerful member of Congress at that time."[10] Dreyfus reported that Norm Ornstein, a veteran political analyst at the conservative American Enterprise Institute in Washington, said: "He has moved more aggressively than anyone I have ever seen to accumulate leverage and power."[11] Dreyfuss further wrote:

> *Yet unlike former speaker Newt Gingrich—who, until his spectacular fall from grace in 1998, was a ubiquitous and controversial symbol of Republican power in the House, and too often excelled as a blue-sky theoretician and strategist—DeLay is nearly faceless, rarely making headlines. DeLay's style is almost the polar opposite of Newt's. He operates largely behind the scenes, pulling strings and making the wheels turn in Congress, and wielding enormous power over the GOP rank and file through a top down command structure of lieutenants. Though fiercely partisan and ideologically bonded to the right wing of the Republican Party, Delay has made himself indispensable by amassing an unparalleled political machine.[12]*

"He is the implementer," says Robert Rusbuldt in the Dreyfuss article, a senior lobbyist for the Independent Insurance Agents of America and a key member of DeLay's "kitchen cabinet." He added, "Some think that he is the enforcer."[13] Nicknamed "the Hammer" for

10   Robert Dreyfuss, "DeLay, Incorporated," *The Texas Observer*, February 4, 2000.

11   Ibid.

12   Ibid.

13   Ibid.

his often heavy-handed use of brute political power, DeLay himself prefers a different and more modest metaphor. Acknowledging that among recent GOP congressional leaders, Speaker Gingrich was the "visionary" and the House majority leader and Dallas Republican Dick Armey was the "policy wonk," DeLay said, "I am the ditch digger who makes it all happen."[14]

DeLay continued to gain power and money. He considered money to be the lifeblood of politics and was the biggest critic of campaign finance reform in Congress. His ability to move people and money around to benefit himself and the Republican Party was significant. The confidence that came with his success caused him to push the envelope of the law more often than he should have, leading to overconfident words and actions. But for now, his strength was intact.

By the summer of 1997, some House Republicans had come to see Gingrich as a liability. Earlier that year, he had become the first Speaker in the history of the House to be disciplined for ethical violations. By a vote of 395–28, he was reprimanded and ordered to pay a $300,000 penalty for ethics violations dating back to 1994.

One violation was related to the use of tax-deductible charitable contributions to finance a college course that Gingrich taught. The Speaker also had given the House ethics committee false information during its investigation.

Several GOP backbenchers—including Steve Largent of Oklahoma, Lindsey Graham of South Carolina, and Mark Souder of Indiana—engineered a conspiracy to replace Gingrich as speaker.

They soon gained the support of four Republicans who ranked directly below Gingrich in the House leadership—Armey, DeLay, Republican Conference chairman John Boehner of Ohio, and Republican Leadership chairman Bill Paxon of New York.

---

14   Ibid.

THE DEATH OF WASHINGTON'S DEMOCRACY?

On July 9, 1997, three of these top guns, DeLay, Boehner, and Paxon had the first of several secret meetings to discuss the rebellion. The next night, DeLay met with twenty of the GOP plotters in Largent's office and appeared to assure them that the leadership (except for the Speaker) was with them.

Under the plotters' plan, Armey, DeLay, Boehner, and Paxon were to present Gingrich with an ultimatum—resign or be voted out. Combined with the votes of the Democrats, there appeared to be enough votes to "vacate the chair," or force the Speaker out of his office.

It was an audacious plan that had all the earmarks of being put together over generous servings of liquor. Then it fell apart.

When the rebels decided that they wanted Paxon to be the new speaker, Armey—who had expected to be rewarded with the job as the next-highest-ranking Republican—became angry. Suddenly, he had no stomach for the ugly intraparty fight because it wouldn't give him a plum promotion. He backed out and told his chief of staff to warn Gingrich about the coup.

Gingrich, in retribution, forced Paxon to resign from his leadership post. The Speaker also wanted to force a vote of confidence in the rest of the Republican leadership but eventually abandoned that idea.

So, DeLay emerged from the aborted coup with his leadership position intact and with a reputation as a fighter for the rank-and-file members of the House.

As majority whip, DeLay earned the nickname "the Hammer" for enforcing strict party discipline in close votes—and for exacting political vengeance on opponents. He obviously preferred that nickname to Hot Tub Tom and pointed out that a hammer is one of a carpenter's most valuable tools.

The Hammer became one of the Republican Party's most valuable tools in Washington. Not only did DeLay use his leadership position to raise outrageous amounts of money for himself and other Republican officeholders and candidates, but he also set what may have been a record in the 104th Congress. He successfully whipped votes on 300 out of 303 bills, a phenomenal—or dictatorial—record, depending on to whom you are talking.

Getting votes is the majority leader's job, and few, if any, majority leaders have tackled it with DeLay's cutthroat enthusiasm. Few Republican House members dared to tell him no, for fear that he would "hammer" their careers by recruiting reelection opponents and arming them to the teeth with special-interest money.

In 1998, Austin's former hot-tubber even succeeded in getting the House to approve articles of impeachment against President Bill Clinton, alleging perjury during the sex scandal involving White House intern Monica Lewinsky and obstruction of justice in a sexual-harassment case claimed by former Arkansas state employee Paula Jones.

DeLay blocked congressional efforts to censure [a lesser action than impeachment] the president because he had a bizarre belief that the U.S. Constitution allowed the House to punish the president only through impeachment.

The controversy created a media circus for weeks, bringing all other work on Capitol Hill to a virtual standstill. Ultimately, the Senate acquitted the president. Senators voted 55–45 against conviction on the perjury charge and split 50–50 on obstruction of justice. A two-thirds majority, or sixty-seven votes, would have been required for conviction and removal of the president from office on either charge. No Democratic senator voted to convict.

At the height of the impeachment controversy, Republicans

lost five seats in the November 1998 elections, prompting Gingrich to announce that he would step down as Speaker. Gingrich had long been a lightning rod, and following the ethics violations, the loss of Republican House seats was viewed as the last straw necessary to end his leadership.

While presiding over the Clinton impeachment, Gingrich also had been having an extramarital affair with a young House staff member, whom he would marry a few years later after divorcing his second wife.

Republicans still held a House majority, but barely. The impeachment effort against Clinton had not increased the Republican margin, as DeLay had promised his GOP colleagues, but had backfired.

Soon, DeLay would be ready to try something else, something just as partisan as the attack against Clinton and even more outrageous.

TEN

TEXAS ON THE GRILL FOR THE NATIONAL GOP

Congressional redistricting is easily one of the most archaic, nuanced components of organizing how citizens in each state are represented in the U.S. House of Representatives.

The Constitution established the House as the branch of government most representative of the nation—and the national mood. Not only are representatives required to run for reelection every two years, but the geographic districts that they represent also are redrawn every ten years (after each U.S. census) to reflect population changes.

At least every ten years is what the Constitution orders in article I, section 2, paragraph 3:

> *Representatives...shall be apportioned among the several States which may be included within this Union, according to their respective numbers....The Actual Enumeration shall be made within...every subsequent Term of ten Years, in such Manner they shall by Law direct.*

James Madison wrote in The Federalist Papers that the House was a "numerous and changeable body." He believed that smaller districts and two-year terms would generate regular turnover, especially compared with the Senate, whose members represent an entire state and serve six-year terms. Two-year terms, Madison believed, would keep House members aware of changes of attitude in their districts.

Even in Madison's day, though, the drawing of House districts wasn't free of efforts to gain partisan or other political advantage. "Gerrymandering," the act of drawing a district to favor a particular political party, group of people, or candidate, was practiced almost from the very beginning of the republic.

There were even claims in the late 1780s that Patrick Henry had tried to gerrymander Madison himself out of the First Congress. The actual term, "gerrymander," was coined during Madison's presidency to mock Elbridge Gerry, the governor of Massachusetts, who, in 1811, approved a district that looked like a salamander.

Compared to today's high-stakes partisan battles over government control, however, those early efforts to distort congressional districts look downright polite.

As a practical matter, Madison's original concept of the House is now outdated. Partisan gerrymandering has become a hyper-precise science, with partisan mapmakers pulling data from census and election returns to design, by computer, the political composition of each congressional district.

"It used to be the idea was that once every two years voters elected their representatives, and, now, instead, it's every 10 years the representatives choose their constituents," Pamela Karlan, a professor at Stanford Law School, told Jeffrey Toobin in The New Yorker.[15]

Central to the art of drawing boundaries for congressional districts is the concept of "communities of interest," or groups of people who have shared interests or backgrounds.

This could include race or ethnicity, a community of interest that was widely violated in the case of minority Americans until a

15   Jeffrey Toobin, "Drawing the Line,: *The New Yorker,*   Citation for Pamela Karlan's comments, March 6, 2006.

series of court decisions and the federal Voting Rights Act ordered minority voting rights protected. No longer is it legally acceptable, as it was for many years, to draw districts in such a fashion as to deliberately minimize the influence of black or Hispanic voters.

Shared interests also could include a common history or culture, a common religion, a shared socio-economic status, or a variety of other ties that create a community of voters with distinct interests.

For example, residents of a rural area wanting to preserve its sparsely populated character might prefer a representative who was opposed to government initiatives that would attract commercial development. Those people constitute a community of interest. Forcing that group to be a part of an unnatural or manufactured area by splitting the rural area, and thereby weakening it, is unfair. Communities should be allowed to develop within themselves based on natural progression.

Another example of a community of interest could be suburban residents with high taxes, who might prefer a congressman who encourages commercial and industrial growth to increase overall tax revenues and relieve their own individual tax burdens. Ideally, they would be in a different congressional district from the rural residents. It is often possible to maintain the integrity of both areas and certainly is much fairer than splitting one and combining it with the other, giving one side of that issue the political advantage over the other.

Traditionally, redistricting did not carve up neighborhoods or divide people who historically had been represented in the same district because of their close geography or shared social and economic interests.

Except for cases in which the courts had ordered some redistricting plans redrawn, congressional redistricting never had been reopened in the middle of a decade simply to give one party partisan advantage over another. Both political parties are guilty of taking advantage of the opportunity to group people together for partisan advantage. In Texas in 2003, the drawings specifically took into the consideration the movement of people from inner cities and into suburbs. As a neighborhood gets older and run-down or changes demographically, the people who can afford it tend to build or buy more modern homes nearby. In some places it might be white flight, but in others it is just new, modern construction.

In Texas, particularly in its major cities, suburbs developed in every case and tended to be more conservative, as it was the affluent who could most easily travel. The less affluent, who tended to vote Democratic, were largely left behind in the city. Those suburbs generally became filled with like-minded conservatives who tended to vote Republican, so when a plan for the boundaries of congressional districts needed to be drawn, it became easy to allow those boundaries to include some of the inner city and then radiate into the suburbs to draw the larger number of Republican voters there into the plan as well. So, while Houston could be easily drawn as a Democratic voting area, dividing Houston into pieces that are individually attached to a Republican voting suburb weakens the Democratic voters while the strengthening the Republican voters. Thus, a crafty politician can "gerrymander" a district to his or her liking. A close inspection of the cities in Texas shows this idea became the rule of the day in 2003. Obviously, there are some exceptions.

One such exception was the effort to get a Republican district in Austin, which has typically voted very Democratic and was represented in Congress by an outspoken progressive named Lloyd Doggett (D-TX). In order to defeat Doggett, a district was drawn to include a portion of Austin, where Doggett lived and represented, and connect it via I-35 to a very heavily concentrated population of

Hispanics almost four hundred miles to the south. The purpose was to concentrate voters into a district that would likely not support Doggett. The Republicans claimed to be creating a minority district intended to be won by a Hispanic candidate. Doggett won anyway, but he had a very difficult time representing that very long and skinny district.

The redistricting timetable and communities of interest protections were soon to be thrown out the window in Texas for the sake of Republican gains—and to help a fiercely partisan Republican congressional leader save face with his colleagues.

* * * *

In 2001, Texas had a Republican governor, Rick Perry, a Republican lieutenant governor, Bill Ratliff, and a Republican majority in the state senate. But Democrats still controlled the Texas House, and the Speaker, Pete Laney, was a Democrat.

That year's legislative session, the first after the 2000 census, was a redistricting session. But the legislature, with each chamber controlled by a different party, was unable to agree on a new redistricting plan for the U.S. House members elected from Texas.

The job then fell to a federal court panel of three judges, all Republican appointees, raising the hopes of Republicans in Austin.

The judges, however, drew a new redistricting map that, after making adjustments for Texas's population changes over the previous decade, maintained the existing 17–15 Democratic majority in the state's congressional delegation. Republicans were furious. They thought they had had an "in" with the judges.

The judges' product was particularly troublesome, and embarrassing, for House Majority Leader Tom DeLay, who had been bragging for several years to his Republican colleagues in

Washington that he could increase the number of Republicans elected to the House from Texas to help the GOP maintain its shaky control of that body. Republicans had a nine-vote majority in the House in 2001, meaning that Democrats needed to capture only five seats from the GOP to reclaim a majority.

The fact that Democrats, despite their other political losses in Texas, still held a majority of the U.S. House delegation from DeLay's home state became a point of weakness for the majority leader with other House Republicans. Whatever grievances some of them had with DeLay, they could routinely count on him to deliver promises involving corporate America or Texas.

He was, after all, the Hammer, the guy who loved to bully people, and usually did so with great effectiveness. With Republican colleagues reminding him of his promises to bolster their slim House majority, DeLay must have come to feel as if his manhood were being questioned.

Never one to mix ethics and politics, or to honor political redistricting tradition, DeLay began conjuring up a new political map of Texas's congressional districts that would replace Democrats with as many Republicans as possible.

At the top of DeLay's Democratic hit list was veteran U.S. Representative Martin Frost, who with Charlie Stenholm shared the distinction of being the longest-serving member of Congress from Texas. Frost's help had been invaluable in my election to Congress. As a member of the House Democratic leadership, Frost frequently butted heads with DeLay, and DeLay truly hated him.

Political tradition, and 230 years of interpreting the Constitution, dictated that redistricting take place once a decade, after the completion of a new census. DeLay was planning a mid-decade blatant power grab.

Early on, DeLay met with Karl Rove, President George W. Bush's chief political adviser and a long-time dark force on the Texas political scene. Not surprisingly, Rove got behind the plan.

Rove had been practicing political dirty tricks since his college days with Lee Atwater in the 1970s. They grew up with the politics of the South, and both were successful in many campaigns. Much of their effectiveness came at the detriment of the Voting Rights Act of 1965. Race played a determining role in their campaigns by using code words and phrases that disguised the racist implications that were important to white southerners. They taught their candidates to use innuendo and insinuation, which leads the target voter to think what he wants and gives the candidate plausible deniability.

On August 10, 1973, as the Watergate scandal raged, the Washington Post reported on tape recordings of Rove conducting training seminars for young Republicans, in which he discussed digging through opponents' garbage cans. The story was headlined "Republican Party Probes Official as Teacher of Tricks."[16]

The FBI questioned the young Rove at President Nixon's request. Former Nixon White House counsel John Dean later said that Watergate prosecutors were interested in Rove's dirty tricks in 1972 but did not pursue him because they had bigger fish to fry.[17]

Fast forward to the twenty-first century, and Rove was still manipulating the body politic.

* * * *

---

16   John Saar, "GOP Probes Official as Teacher if Tricks," *The Washington Post.*, August 10, 1973.

17   Ibid.

THE DEATH OF WASHINGTON'S DEMOCRACY?

In order for DeLay to advance his plan to draw a Republican congressional map, Republicans first had to capture control of the Texas House, a body that had been in Democratic hands for more than a century. Republicans had been steadily chipping away at the Democratic majority for the previous twenty years, but at the end of 2001 Democrats still held a narrow edge. If Republicans could gain a House majority, they would elect a House speaker and control all the power points in state government. The governor and all other statewide elected officials already were Republicans, and the GOP already held a majority of the state senate.

Not only had the Democratic Texas House and the Republican Texas Senate been unable to agree on a congressional redistricting plan in 2001, they also had been unable to pass legislation redrawing their own new legislative districts. And that would prove to be a big boost for the GOP because the Texas Constitution required that, in the event of the legislature's failure, the task of redrawing legislative districts be handed to the Legislative Redistricting Board.

This board included five statewide elected officials—the lieutenant governor, the Speaker, the attorney general, the comptroller, and the land commissioner. All were Republicans except Speaker Pete Laney. With Laney and Lieutenant Governor Bill Ratliff, a moderate Republican, outvoted 3–2, the board drew a new redistricting plan for the Texas House that favored Republican candidates in a number of districts around the state and greatly enhanced the Republicans' chances of capturing a House majority in the 2002 elections. Voting for the new plan were Attorney General John Cornyn, who later was elected to the U.S. Senate; Land Commissioner David Dewhurst, later elected lieutenant governor; and Comptroller Carole Keeton Strayhorn.

Already given a big boost toward his goal, DeLay also

organized Texans for a Republican Majority (TRMPAC), a political action committee designed to raise campaign funds for Republican legislative candidates. It was modeled after his Americans for a Republican Majority (ARMPAC), a highly successful federal committee that had raised money for Republican candidates in the 2000 congressional elections.

DeLay was a virtual money-making machine. It was his most valuable political asset. It was the hand wielding the Hammer. His goal now was to give Republicans a majority of the Texas House in the 2002 elections and remove the last obstacle to full Republican control of state government.

TRMPAC raised $1.5 million, with much of the money coming from outside Texas. Contributing $25,000 was the law firm of Jack Abramoff, a Washington lobbyist who a few years later would be sent to prison after pleading guilty to federal bribery charges. DeLay had described Abramoff as one of his "closest and dearest friends."[18]

TRMPAC helped Republicans secure a majority of the Texas House for the first time since Reconstruction. The committee's activity also would eventually result in civil lawsuits over the use of corporate money and criminal indictments against DeLay and two associates on charges of money laundering and conspiracy.

They were accused of raising $190,000 in corporate money through TRMPAC and then sending that money to the Republican National Committee, which then sent $190,000 to seven Republican legislative candidates. It is illegal under Texas law to donate corporate money to campaigns for elective office, and prosecutors contended that DeLay and his fellow defendants—political consultants John Colyandro and Jim Ellis—used the Republican National Committee to launder corporate donations.

---

18   Michael Grubwald, "DeLay Pulls No Punches in Final Speech in House," The Washington Post, June 9, 2006.

THE DEATH OF WASHINGTON'S DEMOCRACY?

DeLay strongly denied the allegations. But his Achilles' Heel, in his manifest exploitation of every facet of state and federal government, was his carelessness with the law and campaign money. In addition he was arrogant, ruthless and on a reckless path of political manipulation that was breathtaking in its scope, intentions, and execution.

In January 2003, the Texas Legislature convened in Austin with a Republican-controlled Senate and a House with a newly won 88–62 Republican majority. On the first day of the session, veteran legislator Tom Craddick of Midland was elected the first Republican Speaker of modern times. Republican Rick Perry was still in the governor's office.

The lawsuits and criminal charges would come later. At that point, DeLay was ready to make his move for a new redistricting map for national congressional seats.

* * * *

Tom DeLay knew he now had control of the entire government of the state of Texas. They had caused the Texas House of Representatives to change from Democratic control to Republican; the Texas Senate changed from Democratic control to Republican; and the governor's position was held by a Republican. They knew an issue regarding boundaries drawn the way they wanted them to be drawn could be forced through the process. They knew that enough of the extra seats they needed to keep control of the U.S. House of Representatives could be won by gerrymandering enough of the districts to change seven districts in Texas from Democrat to Republican. All of the critical positions were now in place, and all that was left to make this plan a reality was for the artists to come in and craft the districts that would guarantee a majority of Republicans in carefully selected areas of the state of Texas.

In the almost 230-year history of our country this plan had not yet been tried. The Constitution said that new boundaries should be drawn at the end of each decade following the census so that a fair apportionment of citizens could be accomplished. DeLay knew the Constitution did not say it couldn't be done at a time other than at the end of a decade, so why not take the chance? After all, the balance of power in Congress was at stake, and he wanted to win at any cost.

The Republicans of Texas succeeded in their goal and won the districts they sought, but not without great difficulty, much anguish, and expensive court battles that would continue well into the decade and probably for many years to come after that. [In fact, both North Carolina and Texas cases were completed by appellate courts as recently as May of 2017] The challenges would continue, the court battles would be fought, but a new precedent had been set: feel free to reshape the playing field whenever political control can be achieved.

In the ensuing years the GOP scored many more seats in the House elections even though Democrats earned millions more votes in House races than their Republican opponents. In an article in the Washington Post, Professor Jeremy Mayer says gerrymandering distorts democracy.[19] As has already been said, when the representatives can choose their constituents instead of the constituents choosing their representatives, the system will not function as our founding fathers intended. People began to speak out against the egregiousness of this new practice of changing boundaries in the middle of a decade and realized that it was happening contrary to what was written in the Constitution of the United States. In an article in the Washington Post, it was written that President Obama called on lawmakers and the public to take a number of steps "to change the system to reflect our better selves

---

19   Christopher Ingraham, "This is actually what America would look like without gerrymandering," *The Washington Post,* January 13, 2016.

for a better politics." The top item on that list was to end partisan gerrymandering: "We have to end the practice of drawing our congressional districts so that politicians can pick their voters, and not the other way around," Obama said.[20]

The Washington Post further wrote that advocates of reform have proposed various solutions to the egregious example of some states gerrymandering in the form that Texas started in 2003, and followed in many other states. Christopher Ingraham in the Washington Post wrote that "in some states, redistricting is put in the hands of an independent commission. And others like the legislative and court battles that are playing out in drawing the districts more fairly to each one's way of thinking. But a fundamental problem with district drawing still remains: as long as humans are drawing the lines, there's a danger of bias and self-interest to creep into the process. There is another way, however; we could simply let computers do the drawing for us."[21] Ingraham proposes that the work of a software engineer in Massachusetts named Brian Olson be considered as a solution.

Ingraham writes that "Olson's algorithm creates 'optimally compact' equal population congressional districts in each state, based on...census data. It draws districts that respect the boundaries of census blocks, which is the smallest geographical unit used for the Census Bureau. This ensures that the district boundaries reflect actual neighborhoods and don't, say, cut an arbitrary line through somebody's house."[22]

As an example, the following maps of the United States were published in the Washington Post. The top map reflects actual congressional districts that have been used in recent elections. The

---

20   Ibid.
21   Ibid.
22   Ibid.

second map reflects the compact districts drawn by Olson's technologically driven plan.[23]

Current congressional district map

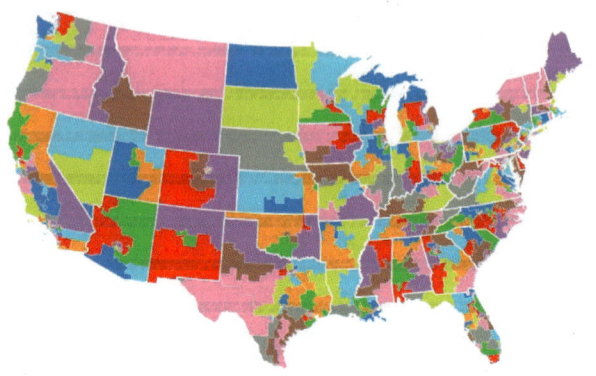

Computer-drawn map to optimize compactness

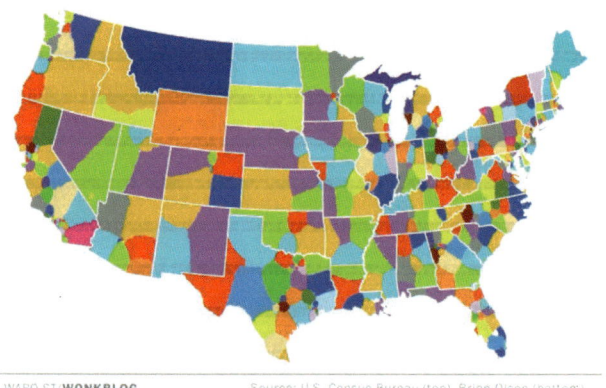

WAPO ST/**WONKBLOG**   Source: U.S. Census Bureau (top), Brian Olson (bottom)

The difference is notable. But it is still more important to consider the impact on the people seeking representation than on what the districts look like or the impact the boundaries have on the politicians. The greater the manipulation, the lower the participation. Our goal should be to encourage, not discourage, participation in the electoral process. The better a representative understands the needs and interests

23   Ibid. Maps appear in Ingraham article.

of a community, the better the representative and the people can address those needs. As President Washington alluded, if you create a system where the power of the individual or the individual's party is more important than Congress, the system will not work.

Even the following map of Texas[24] will function better than the squiggly lines and four-hundred-mile-long districts that have been used to manipulate the future of politics purely for partisan gain. The point is, there are options to the political manipulation, gerrymandering, of something that is as important as a person's vote, and our goal should be the empowerment of that vote in every way possible. It is unfortunate that the Texans, Tom DeLay, Karl Rove, and others, who were seeking immediate gratification and power for themselves and their party could not see far enough into the future as George Washington did in his effort to create a better world for coming generations of Americans.

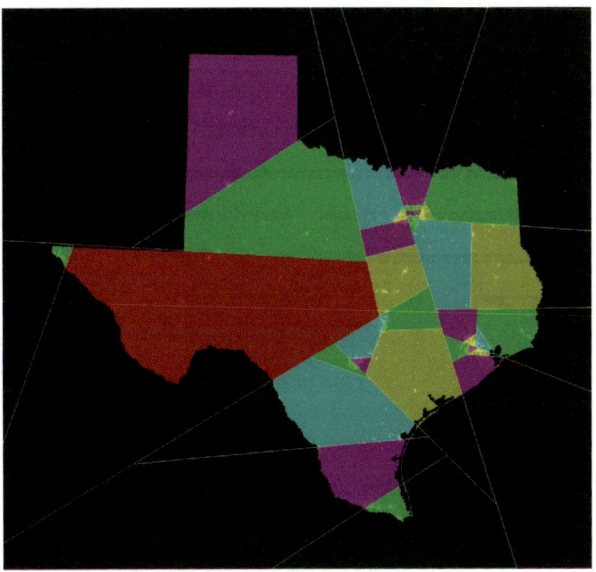

---

24   Map of Texas with adjusted districts,
        http://rangevoting.org/Splitline2009/tx.png.

ELEVEN

The Fight Is On

On February 12, 2003, Tom DeLay, continuing as the majority leader of the U.S. House of Representatives, hosted a dinner for his fellow House members from Texas and their spouses in the Columbus Room at Washington's historic Union Station. There were no other attendees, not even staff members, which was a little unusual for such congressional gatherings.

Addressing the bipartisan group, DeLay hearkened back to the days when Democratic speakers from Texas, Sam Rayburn and Jim Wright, had all lawmakers from Texas, Democrats and Republicans alike, working together on behalf of their state. Those may have been the only true words he spoke that night.

As recently as the 1970s and 1980s, the Texas delegation had been legendary in the U.S. House for its bipartisan cohesion. If a congressman from Texas had an issue in a committee on which he didn't sit, another Texan of either party on the committee would help without hesitation.

But since Newt Gingrich, Tom DeLay, and their Republican revolutionaries had "burned down" the House, that level of cooperation and bipartisanship on behalf of DeLay's home state also was now in ashes.

Nevertheless, DeLay had the audacity to call us together, ostensibly for a social function, and pretend to play statesman. His motives were not unlike those of the World War II Japanese "diplomats," who professed to be working for peace in Washington as their country's leaders back home were planning the surprise, deadly attack on Pearl Harbor.

DeLay's message that night was that we should all work together for the greater good of Texas. Exchanging glances, we Democrats in the audience could barely disguise our smirks.

Democrat Martin Frost sat for as long as he could without laughing. Then he stood up and said, "Tom, how in the world do you expect us to 'work together' here in DC while you are stalking us with knives in Texas, trying to defeat us by redistricting coup? How exactly do we do that? There's no reservoir of trust here." We fellow Democrats nodded our heads as our wives squirmed in their seats, visibly uncomfortable.

DeLay's demeanor changed visibly. His face reddened, and he seemed to be holding his temper. There wasn't much more of an exchange between audience and host after that. And, the alleged social event—a social event designed to mask the political attack that DeLay already was organizing in Austin against us Democrats—was over.

DeLay was embarrassed that his stunt had thudded so badly. He must have really believed that his little song and dance was going to fool all of us and camouflage his backstabbing scheme in Texas.

DeLay went back to the Capitol and, speaking on the fate of a controversial judicial nominee under consideration in the Senate, made the most partisan, rank, offensive remarks we had ever heard delivered in the well of the House.

Democrats opposed Republicans, he ranted, because of the "intellectually dishonest tenets of an all-consuming leftist ideology that is driven entirely by an appetite to destroy anyone standing beyond its control.

"The left is inflamed by any prospective judicial candidate with the courage to oppose their unrelenting, small-minded, intolerant hostility to the traditional foundations of American life: faith in God, reverence for tradition, respect for the true rule of law and the recognition that we are all ultimately accountable for our actions," he continued.

"That last point in particular, Mr. Speaker, summons the deepest venom and bile from the left," he added. "They attempted over the four decades beginning in the 1960s to put forth a vast and sordid swindle upon the American people. The left claim that they could ignore our most sacred and sacrosanct traditions, that in service of convenience, they could callously destroy and step forward without consequences."[25]

DeLay had quickly returned to his standard script: Republicans good, Democrats evil. This was an immature view of only seeing things in black and white with no shades of gray: my way is the only way. It seemed we had turned a corner and were battening down the hatches for the fight to come.

* * * *

The month before DeLay's fake olive-branch dinner in Washington, Frost had run into DeLay in Austin, where the majority leader was already lobbying key Republicans for his mid-decade redistricting scheme.

"Tom, I know what you're doing here," Frost told him. DeLay replied that the two of them, as congressional leaders of their respective parties, could hammer out a new redistricting map together. DeLay said he needed Frost to give up two Democratic

---

25   Tom DeLay, The Congressional Record, "Senate Confirmation of Miguel Estrada", *The Congressional Record,* February 12, 2003

seats, which would switch a 17–15 Democratic majority for Texas in the U.S. House to a 17–15 Republican majority.

Frost rejected the offer. "Thanks, Tom, but the Democrats will sink or swim together," he said.

* * * *

On the eve of the epic 2003 redistricting fight, Democrats and Republicans both underestimated the other. Democrats never figured the Republicans would go to such enormous lengths to impose a new congressional map on Texas. They hadn't planned on DeLay using legally questionable campaign-finance tactics to help give the Republicans a critical majority—and the speakership—of the Texas House.

They didn't count on DeLay convincing state Republican leaders to reopen redistricting mid-decade and didn't anticipate one key legislative rule being changed to eventually facilitate passage of the new map. And they didn't anticipate the Republican abuse of federal agencies, including the Federal Aviation Administration and the U S Department of Justice, which was to come during the redistricting saga.

Republicans, meanwhile, never figured the Democrats would fight so mightily—both conventionally and unconventionally—as they were to do against the power grab. But Democrats treated the drawn-out fight as the political campaign that it was.

* * * *

The Texas Legislature, with a new Republican majority and Republican Speaker in the House, began the 2003 regular legislative session in January facing a ton of issues of critical importance to Texans—education, health care, insurance regulation, and protecting Texas military bases from an upcoming round of base closures.

Lawmakers also had to contend with a $10 billion revenue shortfall, prompting a struggle between Democrats and Republicans over budget priorities. The Republicans ultimately would prevail by making deep cuts in important state services, including health care for children, and removing legislative restraints on university tuition.

One thing legislators didn't have to do was redraw congressional district lines. They had failed to accomplish that task in 2001, the first session after the 2000 census, and had let the federal courts do it for them, as the U S Constitution intended.

Redistricting was not a "do-over" proposition, at least not until DeLay and other Texas Republican leaders decided to increase their partisan clout in a way outside the election process. Their 2003 redistricting drive was about power—power not awarded at the ballot box.

Many Democrats in the legislature fought hard against that power grab, even though the numbers weren't on their side. There was precedence for Texans taking on battles where we were outnumbered! [Remember the Alamo] The Republicans were in for a Texas-sized surprise. Traditional checks and balances were not working, with the courts or laws and leadership acting politically rather than judicially. This was war!

One of the early fighters was state representative Richard Raymond of Laredo, the senior Democrat on the House Redistricting Committee, who stood up to state representative Joe Crabb of Kingwood, the Republican committee chairman.

As Crabb tried to ram DeLay's plan through committee, Raymond recited, in methodical and painstaking detail, the examples of illegality and pure obsession inherent in the plan and what its adoption would mean to Texas. Raymond meticulously listed each instance of abuse of power, disenfranchisement of minority voters, and other constitutional violations.

But as hard as they fought, Raymond and his fellow Democrats in the Texas House were unable to keep the redistricting plan bottled up in committee. Late in the 2003 regular session, on May 12 to be exact, the plan was scheduled for a vote on the House floor, where Democrats were outnumbered, 88–62.

TWELVE

EMULATING ABE LINCOLN

One day in 1840, while a member of the Illinois legislature, Abraham Lincoln found himself in the minority on a political issue, and he found the spot so uncomfortable that he did something rather surprising about it.

He climbed out a window of the meeting hall, his long legs momentarily dangling before he dropped from the window ledge to the ground below, and hurried away.

Yes, the future president who would lead the Union to victory and preserve the United States during the dark days of the Civil War avoided a more mundane political fight during his younger years by bolting from a showdown.

Was he being a coward? No, he was breaking a quorum and preventing a vote that he didn't want to see take place. He and his Whig colleagues (he would become a Republican later) were involved in a banking dispute with Democratic legislators, and on that particular day the Whigs had been outnumbered. The normal exit was blocked by a doorman, but the window was available.

Breaking a quorum, the so-called nuclear option for a legislative minority, is rarely used, and when it is, it is usually controversial and often unsuccessful. It is a last resort for legislators who would lose if a vote on a particularly important issue were taken. So, they prevent the vote by boycotting work and depriving the legislative body of a quorum—the minimum number of lawmakers who must be present for the body to conduct business.

In the case of the Texas Legislature, a quorum is two-thirds of the membership of the House or the Senate.

The most famous, successful use of the tactic in Texas occurred in 1979, when a dozen moderate-to-liberal Democratic state senators—dubbed the "Killer Bees"—boycotted the Senate for several days to prevent a vote on a controversial presidential primary bill being pushed by then lieutenant governor Bill Hobby.

The Texas Senate was firmly under Democratic control in those days, and the fight was between conservative and liberal factions of the party. Hobby and the remaining senators put a "call" on the Senate, which authorized state troopers to search for the missing senators and, if they found them, bring them back to the Texas State Capitol.

Although most of the boycotting senators were hiding in a garage apartment in west Austin, only a short drive from the capitol, they remained undetected until Hobby agreed to let the bill die.

Twenty-four years later, with Republicans in control of the Texas Legislature and a Republican-drafted congressional redistricting bill ready for certain House approval, fifty-one Democratic state representatives decided to exercise the "nuclear" option.

Taking no chances that some of their large number would be found and forced to return to the capitol—fifty-one is the minimum number required to break a quorum in the 150-member House—these Democrats didn't try to hide in Austin, or anywhere in Texas for that matter.

On Sunday evening, May 11, 2003, Mother's Day, they headed for Ardmore, Oklahoma, where they "hid" in plain sight just across the state line and outside the jurisdiction of Texas law-enforcement officers. Following a careful secret plan, most traveled by chartered buses from Austin. A few drove their own cars and one, former Speaker Pete Laney, flew in his private plane, a seven-seat Piper Cheyenne, from his rural home in West Texas.

Preparations had involved a lot of spying and intelligence gathering. Even those who organized the effort were not sure how many of the Democrats would actually get on the buses.

Bear in mind, Texas is a deeply conservative state, and Republicans were in charge of the legislature. Each lawmaker who chose to participate in the boycott had to weigh his or her own constituents' reactions as well as retribution from then Speaker Tom Craddick, an autocratic Republican who could punish them by killing legislative priorities important to their constituents.

Democrats who were loyal to Craddick, the so-called Craddick Ds, had been left out of the planning, and they were as surprised by the boycott as were the Republicans.

Ardmore offered only modest hotel accommodations and other sparse amenities, and that was one reason—plus its proximity— that it had been chosen by the boycotting Democrats. They didn't want constituents back home to think they had set off on a "fun vacation" during the critical closing days of a legislative session.

Craddick and the remaining House members, when they convened on Monday, May 12, had arrest warrants issued for the missing lawmakers, but the warrants were worthless in Oklahoma.

The boycotting Democrats, who became known as the "Killer Ds," remained at the Ardmore Holiday Inn, dining at an adjoining Denny's, for four days, through May 15, the last day that new House bills, including the redistricting plan, could be considered by the House during the 2003 regular session. With the bill dead, they returned home to a heroes' welcome from their fellow partisans.

They had won an important battle, but the war wasn't over. In both Washington and Austin, Republican leaders were prepared to abuse their authority and bend the rules to replace duly elected Democrats with Republicans in Congress. Resorting to such tactics was a common strategy for them. I guess they didn't care about the lesson I learned as a child: Going to any extreme to get your way doesn't make for good family interaction.

Tom DeLay, the majority leader of the U.S. House and the architect of the redistricting scheme, already was treating the federal government as if it were a branch of the Republican Party. On the afternoon of May 12, before the missing Democrats' location had become known, a senior aide to DeLay called an official with the Federal Aviation Administration (FAA) and asked the agency to track the location of a plane with tail number N711RD. It was Pete Laney's plane. The staffer didn't say why he wanted the information, and FAA officials later said they had assumed there was a safety issue involving the aircraft.[26] But DeLay, of course, was trying to locate the Democrats, and the only safety issue—if there was one—involved his blood pressure.

The inspector general of the U.S. Department of Homeland Security also revealed later that a DeLay staffer had contacted his agency "requesting assistance in determining the location of an aircraft believed to be overdue."[27] By the end of the day, the FAA had told DeLay's staff that local officials had traced the plane to Ardmore, Oklahoma.

The same day, DeLay's staff also contacted a senior official at the U.S. Department of Justice, asking whether federal law enforcement authorities would assist in arresting the missing legislators. The department's inspector general later issued a report

26   R. G. Ratcliffe and Karen Masterson, "DeLay admits to role in hunting Democrats", *Houston Chronicle,* May 23, 2003.

27   Ibid.

saying that another justice official had concluded that the request was "wacko" and that the department had refused to get involved.[28]

On June 30, about a month after the regular session had ended, Governor Rick Perry called the legislature back to Austin for a special session that he and DeLay hoped would finish the work on the new congressional map.

With the Democratic representatives back in the state and Republicans holding an 88–62 majority, the House approved DeLay's plan. This time, however, the bill died in the Senate, the victim of that body's "two-thirds rule."

Republicans had a 19–12 Senate majority, but the two-thirds rule, a Senate tradition for many years, required two-thirds of the body to suspend a procedural rule before any bill could be debated on the Senate floor. That meant that only eleven senators could block debate on any piece of legislation, and that's exactly what the Democratic bloc of senators did for the remainder of the special session, which was limited by the state constitution to thirty days' duration.

There is no constitutional limit, however, on the number of special sessions a governor can call, and Perry prepared to call a second special session on the heels of the first. Moreover, Republican Lieutenant Governor David Dewhurst, who presided over the Senate, served notice that he and Republican senators would bypass the two-thirds rule for the next session and allow the redistricting bill to be debated on a simple majority vote.

Dewhurst had resisted Republican pressure to abandon the two-thirds rule during the first special session, but he felt he could no longer hold out. The partisan heat was rising, and Dewhurst had visions of moving up to higher office, notably governor, someday. He couldn't afford to continue antagonizing his party's rabid partisans.

---

28   Jeffrey Toobin, "Drawing the Line: Will Tom DeLay's redistricting in Texas cost him his seat?" *The New Yorker,* March 6, 2006.

He also was visited about that time by Karen Hughes, longtime adviser to President George W. Bush. I don't know how much pressure the White House was exerting on Bush and the Texas Senate. But Karl Rove, the president's chief political adviser, who was an early collaborator with DeLay on the redistricting scheme, was also making calls, pushing for a new Republican congressional map.

One Rove call went to State Senator Bill Ratliff of Mount Pleasant, one of two Republican senators known to be undecided about the new redistricting effort.

Later, Hughes—in the public campaign for redistricting—complained that her congressman, Democrat Lloyd Doggett of Austin, didn't represent her views in Washington. She had to be reminded by a reporter that her congressman wasn't Doggett. It was Republican Lamar Smith.

DeLay and Republican state leaders argued that it was only right to redraw the congressional districts to favor Republican candidates because every statewide elected official in Austin was a Republican and Republicans held majorities in both houses of the legislature.   A Republican majority in the state's congressional delegation would better reflect the partisan makeup of Texas, they claimed.

The real reason, however, was simply to help Republicans hang on to their narrow majority in the U.S. House and save face for DeLay. The whole thing was anathema to the very spirit of democracy, and I was offended—not only because my congressional seat had a big bull's-eye on it, but also because it was just plain wrong.

Polls showed that 82 percent of the people of Texas also thought that what the Republicans were doing was wrong. But fighting DeLay as members of a minority party was like taking on an armed guard with a plastic spoon.

Governor Rick Perry also gets a large share of the blame for the redistricting brouhaha and for putting state business behind the personal political outrages of Tom DeLay. Perry could have stopped the partisan manipulation of the Texas Legislature by refusing to call any special sessions. Instead, he encouraged the partisanship and helped further DeLay's cause.

A coarse sign carried in protest outside the Texas Governor's Mansion during the redistricting fight accurately summed up Governor Perry's relationship with the then U.S. House majority leader. The sign famously declared: "DeLay's Bitch." This was a very bad and misdirected case on Perry's part of follow-the-leader.

Perry's part in this monumental abuse of authority—he would call three special sessions in all—brought him the infamy of the redistricting plan being labeled as "Perrymandering," the twenty-first-century equivalent of "gerrymandering."

On July 28, 2003, the same day that the governor was preparing to issue a proclamation calling the second special session, eleven of the Senate's twelve Democrats quietly slipped away from the Texas State Capitol or their apartments and headed for the Austin airport, where two private planes provided by supporters awaited them.

The House Democrats' flight to Ardmore several weeks earlier had some news reporters and probably some Republican senators anticipating a similar move by Democratic senators. But by the time their absence from the capitol had become obvious, they were already airborne, accompanied by only one staffer, Harold Cook, from the Senate's Democratic caucus.

So secret was their planning that the eleven fleeing Senators didn't even know their destination until after they were in the air.

They hadn't been gone very long when a Houston Chronicle reporter at the Texas State Capitol got a call on his cell phone. He answered to hear a hoarse-sounding voice saying in a whisper, "This is Mario." It was Democratic State Senator Mario Gallegos of Houston, calling from one of the planes. The senator kept the call very short. But he told the reporter all he needed to know for the time being.

"It's Albuquerque. We're going to Albuquerque," Gallegos said, before hanging up.

* * * *

I don't know how long the Texas senators thought they would be on the lam when they checked in later that afternoon at a Marriott Hotel in Albuquerque. They had killed a Senate quorum, but, unlike Ardmore, this was no four-day proposition. A thirty-day special session was just beginning, and there was no limit on the number of special sessions that Perry could call.

Being a state senator is a part-time job, paying $7,200 a year, and they were going to be paying their own expenses in Albuquerque. How long could they afford to be away from their law firms and other primary sources of income back home? How long would they want to be away from their families? Even a short visit to their homes or business offices in Texas would put them at risk of being discovered, arrested by law enforcement officers, and returned to the Texas State Capitol.

The senators had managed to pack some bags before leaving Austin, but one of their first items of business in Albuquerque was a shopping excursion, Cook told a New York Times reporter who visited the Texans a couple of days after their arrival in New Mexico.

"We had to make a Wal-Mart run, because one senator forgot

his belt and his pants were falling down, and some people had forgotten cell phone batteries and underwear and stuff like that. It was the biggest mess," Cook said.[29]

Senator Gonzalo Barrientos had left his wallet in Austin and had to call home for a cash transfer.

Senator Eddie Lucio Jr. of Brownsville had suffered a heart attack and undergone surgery in June, but his cardiologist in Texas arranged for a colleague in Albuquerque to care for the senator.

New Mexico governor Bill Richardson, a Democrat, dropped by the hotel the day after the Texans' arrival to welcome them to his state and applaud their fight against "raw political maneuvering."

Senator Leticia Van de Putte of San Antonio, chair of the Texas Senate Democratic Caucus, called the mid-decade redistricting effort a "partisan power grab." She said the Democrats would return to Austin if redistricting were dropped from the agenda or if the Senate leadership decided to once again honor the traditional two-thirds rule, which would have allowed the Democrats to block further action on a redistricting bill, as they had during the first special session.[30]

The only Democratic senator who didn't flee to New Mexico was State Senator Ken Armbrister of Victoria, a veteran, conservative lawmaker whose district, he said, was more Republican than some of the senatorial districts represented by Republicans. Armbrister would retire from the Senate three years later and join Governor Perry's staff.

* * * *

---

29   Nick Madigan, "On the Lam, Texas Democrats Rough It," *New York Times*, August 1, 2003, mobile.nytimes.com

30   "The Texas Stalemate: It's All About Race," Michelle Goldberg, September 3, 2003, www.salon.com/2003/09/03/texas_18/

The second special session was essentially over before it ever began because the eleven Democratic senators remained in Albuquerque, where they were covered extensively by the Texas and national media, for more than a month. There was an almost daily barrage of political charges and countercharges flying across the state line between the Texas Democrats in Albuquerque and the Texas Republicans in Austin.

Texas Senate Republicans even revoked the capitol parking privileges of Democratic staffers in Austin and fined the absent senators thousands of dollars, fines that no one ever attempted to collect.

DeLay, Perry, Dewhurst, and Republican senators argued that the Democratic majority in the Texas congressional delegation didn't represent the strong Republican majority in Texas. The Republican leaders contended that redrawing the district lines not only would increase the number of Republicans in Congress, but it also would create a couple of new districts for minorities. But that justification was weak because the re-districting plan would be at the expense of moderate, Anglo Democratic incumbents who had been very sensitive to minority concerns.

Nine of the eleven state senators in Albuquerque were minorities, seven Hispanics and two African Americans, and the other two represented districts dominated by minority constituents. They didn't buy the argument that Republicans had the best interests of minority Texans in mind.

"If you look at their voting records, you will see a stark difference in how (Anglo) representatives from the two parties vote on black and Hispanic issues," Democratic Senator Judith Zaffirini of Laredo, a Hispanic, told a reporter for Salon.com while in Albuquerque. "Redistricting is a weapon of mass discrimination," she said.[31]

---

31   Ibid.

Hispanic and African American voters in Texas vote overwhelmingly for Democratic candidates, and the two groups combined were rapidly becoming a majority of the Texas population. The Republicans, by gerrymandering the congressional districts, were desperately trying to extend their hold on power in the face of a changing demographic and political wave.

They also were playing the race card, trying to marginalize the Democratic Party as a party for minorities in order to drive more moderate Anglo Democrats into the Republican fold. It was part of the southern strategy pioneered years earlier by Richard Nixon and enthusiastically embraced by Karl Rove.

* * * *

Throughout that summer, the Texas Democrats in the U.S. House including me convened daily in Martin Frost's Washington office to brainstorm, to find ways to support our legislative colleagues in Albuquerque in our mutual cause of protecting Texas voters.

One day, I ran into the meeting room early, animated over the latest DeLay-inspired injustice, and vented with a couple of staffers.

"If this thing goes through, I want to get first shot at running against DeLay," I huffed.

Instantly, the others in the room—to a person—stood up and pulled wrinkled bills and loose change out of their pockets and put them on a chair in front of me. Some even threw the money down defiantly.

"That's why I want first dibs," I laughed. "Wouldn't have any trouble raising money."

* * * *

"The Albuquerque Democrats might as well learn the Ballad of the Alamo because no reinforcements are coming and they're running out of ammunition," R. G. Ratcliffe wrote in the Houston Chronicle on Monday, September 1, Labor Day.[32]

The article was prophetic because one of the Democrats, Senator John Whitmire of Houston, also had run out of patience with his life in exile and unbeknownst to his colleagues was ready to leave Albuquerque.

The second special session had ended the previous week, on August 26, after reaching its constitutional limit of thirty days, and Governor Perry hadn't said yet—at least publicly—when he would call an anticipated third session.

On August 27, some of the senators returned to Texas to attend a hearing on a last-gasp lawsuit they had filed in federal district court in Laredo. The lawsuit alleged that the Senate's abandonment of the two-thirds rule had amounted to a change in election procedures requiring preclearance by the U.S. Department of Justice under the Voting Rights Act.

After hearing the claim, U.S. District Judge George P. Kazen, a Democratic appointee, didn't immediately issue a ruling, but he expressed strong doubts about the Democrats' claim.

The following weekend was Labor Day weekend, and several senators made plans to leave Albuquerque for the holiday and return the following Tuesday.

Unbeknownst to his colleagues, Whitmire returned to Houston, where he visited with many of his supporters and constituents over the holiday weekend. He also talked with Lieutenant Governor

---

32   Ibid.

Dewhurst before returning to Albuquerque on Tuesday, September 2, to pack up and inform the other senators that he was going back to Texas—to stay. And, he did, later that same day.

Whitmire, who earlier had acknowledged being "homesick," said it was pointless and a waste of energy to continue the boycott because there was no realistic route to a Democratic victory.

"We cannot remain in New Mexico indefinitely," he said in an interview with the New York Times after returning to Houston. He said he still strongly opposed the redistricting "power grab" but would now fight it on the floor of the Senate.[33]

Democrats knew a fight on the Texas Senate floor was a lost cause, and the remaining state senators in Albuquerque—as well as many of their supporters in Texas and Washington—were angry and disappointed. One Democratic senator said he felt "betrayed."[34]

We Democratic congressmen whose districts—and political futures—were on the line were also furious. From Washington, we had been eagerly cheering the boycotters on, but now one was giving up. If words could kill, Whitmire would not have made it back to Texas.

There was speculation that Whitmire, who was counsel to the Dallas-based Locke Lord Bissell & Liddell law firm, had yielded to pressure from the firm, which had strong ties to President Bush. Bush's chief political adviser, Karl Rove, was in the middle of the redistricting scheme with DeLay, and the president obviously was interested in seeing more Republicans elected to Congress.

Jeff Love, chairman of Locke Lord's Houston office, was a Bush "pioneer" in both 2000 and 2004, meaning he raised at least $100,000 for each of the president's campaigns.

33   Kirk Semple, "Texas Democrats Return to Face Redistricting Plan," *The New York Times,* September 15, 2003.

34   Ibid.

Another significant player, Harriet Miers—Bush's longtime lawyer, White House assistant, and short-lived (in 2005) nominee to the U.S. Supreme Court—had been a former managing partner of one of Locke Lord's predecessor firms and, after leaving the White House in 2007, returned to Locke Lord. Another Locke Lord partner, Karin B. Torgerson, also held several positions at the White House from 2003 to 2005.

Whitmire denied the law firm had anything to do with his decision to return to Texas.

"My law firm and my politics are totally separate," he was quoted in the Houston Press a few days after ending his exile. "Look how I vote and see if you think it's influenced by anyone other than the district I represent."[35]

In Washington, his good friend Democratic Representative Gene Green tried to calm the rest of us Democratic congressmen down, and ultimately we relented. But we all felt Whitmire was the guy who did us in and gave the victory to the Republicans.

Whitmire's return to Texas broke the back of the boycott because his presence in the Senate during a third special session would restore a quorum enabling the Republicans to act on a redistricting plan. Even if he didn't go to Austin voluntarily, his presence in Texas made him subject to arrest and being forced to attend the session.

The other ten senators, nevertheless, continued their boycott for a while longer. They had become political heroes to Democrats in Washington and across the country, and some national Democrats tried to use their celebrity to inject some early energy into the 2004 Democratic presidential campaign.

---

35   Tim Fleck, "Return of the Boogie Man," *Houston Press,* September 11, 2003

.

Presidential hopefuls Howard Dean, Dick Gephardt, and Joe Lieberman visited the Texas state senators in Albuquerque while the candidates were in town for a Democratic debate. Some of the state senators went to Washington to meet with Texas Democratic congressmen and the news media. And several appeared at rallies around the country on a Democratic tour sponsored by MoveOn.org.

But time was running out.

* * * *

On September 9, Governor Perry announced that he would call a third special session to convene September 15. And, on September 12, a three-judge federal panel, which included Judge Kazen and two Republican appointees, unanimously dismissed the Democratic senators' lawsuit over the two-thirds rule.

Whitmire showed up voluntarily for the third special session. And so, defiantly, did the other ten former exiles. But, ironically, now that the Republicans had the Democratic lawmakers where they wanted them—forming a quorum back in Austin—the Republicans still had trouble closing the deal on a new redistricting map. This time, though, the fight was among themselves.

The main dispute was between House Speaker Tom Craddick and several other Republican legislators over how to redraw the district lines in West Texas. Craddick was insistent that a new congressional district be created in such a fashion that it be dominated by his hometown, Midland. Determined that his redistricting effort wouldn't be denied again, Tom DeLay went to Austin to help Republicans hammer out a final compromise that gave Craddick what he wanted.

Voting along party lines, the Texas House approved the final plan on October 10. The Senate approved it on October 12. The Senate vote was 17–14. All twelve Democrats, including the nonboycotting Ken Armbrister, voted against it. So did two Republicans, Bill Ratliff of Mount Pleasant and Troy Fraser of Horseshoe Bay.

Governor Perry signed the bill into law the next day, October 13.

THIRTEEN

A SCORCHED POLITICAL LANDSCAPE

At a 2003 White House briefing, reporters asked Tom DeLay if he had discussed his Texas redistricting bill with President George W. Bush and his political adviser, Karl Rove.

"They just congratulated...Texas," DeLay replied with a cynical smile, his long pause implying that the president and Rove had actually congratulated DeLay.

There was nothing in the redistricting outcome for which to congratulate Texas, a state that soon would forfeit eighty-six years of invaluable congressional seniority and experience simply because it had been held by Democrats, lawmakers who had been vetted repeatedly by Texas voters.

The congressmen may have been important to their constituents, but they weren't part of Tom DeLay's partisan restructuring efforts in Texas and on the national stage.

After the new redistricting plan had been signed by Governor Perry, Joby Fortson, a political aide to Texas Republican representative Joe Barton, sent a candid e-mail to a group of colleagues, laying bare the Republicans' naked intentions. The memo, disclosed in subsequent litigation and shared by Congressman Martin Frost with several of his Democratic colleagues, offered a quick rundown on the disposition of each of the seats in the delegation.

The email indicated Fortson was laughing at the fact that the district of Martin Frost of Dallas, the senior Democrat in the state, had disappeared. The memo noted that a GOP incumbent and Frost were drawn together in a Republican district. Fortson bragged that this is the most aggressive map he had ever seen and that it will have a real national impact that should assure that Republicans keep the House no matter the national mood.

This was the first time we heard any of the Texas Republicans spew publicly what we knew they had been saying privately all along: Texas was big enough to reconfigure to create enough Republican seats to ensure that the GOP retained its slim majority in the U.S. House.

Fortson also noted that DeLay gave away enough Rs [(Republicans)] to help his neighboring Republican congressman, Ron Paul. As a result, DeLay was reelected in 2004 with only 55 percent of the vote against an underfunded and unknown Democratic opponent, even though his district voted 67 percent Republican in the presidential race that year. It should have been a warning bell for the fading Republican leader.

The redistricting plan targeted ten white Democratic incumbents. In addition to Frost and me, they were Max Sandlin of Marshall, Jim Turner of Crockett, Ralph Hall of Rockwall, Lloyd Doggett of Austin, Chet Edwards of Waco, Charles Stenholm of Stamford, and Chris Bell and Gene Green of Houston.

It also sought to neutralize Hispanic Democrat Ciro Rodriguez of San Antonio by putting much of Webb County (Laredo) in his district. This was done to protect Hispanic Republican congressman Henry Bonilla of San Antonio, who had survived a stiff challenge from conservative Democrat Henry Cuellar of Laredo in 2002. The idea was to encourage Cuellar to run against Rodriguez instead in 2004, which he did, successfully unseating the incumbent in the Democratic primary and later winning the general election.

* * * *

After Perry signed the redistricting plan, the fight over the new districts continued on two legal tracks. One: the state's lawyers prepared to submit the new plan for approval by the U.S. Department of Justice Civil Rights Division, where the wheels already had been greased for the Republicans by a political crony of President Bush. Two: Texas Democrats filed a lawsuit in federal court, seeking to overturn or block the new district lines.

The Voting Rights Act, initially enacted on the federal level in 1965 and expanded to Texas ten years later, was designed to protect the voting rights of minorities. It requires Texas and other states with a history of discriminatory election practices to submit changes in their voting systems or election maps to the Department of Justice Civil Rights Division or the federal district court in Washington for approval.

Up until the 1960s, the conservative Texas Democrats who ran state government imposed a series of discriminatory election practices designed to discourage Hispanics and African Americans from voting. For many years, until struck down by the federal courts, there even was a "white primary," which prohibited minorities from voting in the only election that really counted in those days, the Democratic primary.

The Democrats' lawsuit was heard by a three-judge federal panel, two of whose members had been appointed by Republican presidents. The panel ruled that the new districts didn't weaken the voting power of African Americans or Hispanics in Texas.

Democrats appealed, and on January 6, 2004, another three-judge panel—this one part of the Fifth U.S. Circuit Court of Appeals—also dismissed the Democrats' claims. But the appellate court criticized the method used by Republicans to reach their political objective.

"We decide only the legality of [the redistricting plan], not its wisdom," the appellate judges wrote. "Whether the Texas Legislature has acted in the best interest of Texas is a judgment that belongs to the people who elected the officials whose act is challenged in this case."[36]

The appellate panel said the decision to move congressional district lines that had been in place for only two years created a strong potential for abuse. "Congress can assist by banning mid-decade redistricting, which it has the clear constitutionality to do, as many states have done," the panel wrote.[37]

Democrats appealed the Fifth Circuit's decision to the U.S. Supreme Court, which eventually would order some limited changes in the plan. But that process would take two more years. So, the Fifth Circuit's ruling and the U.S. Department of Justice's approval meant all the new, Republican-drawn districts would stand for the 2004 elections.

* * * *

During President George W. Bush's administration, the U.S. Department of Justice was widely referred to as the "Just Us Department," because the president and his inner circle filled it with cronies who took unfair and unethical advantage of national resources for their own political causes and benefit. Thanks to one of those partisan cronies, an influential lawyer named Hans von Spakovsky, the department was Tom DeLay's handmaiden in the redistricting travesty.

---

36   Fifth Circuit Court of Appeals, Democratic Party versus State of Texas, January 6, 2004

37   Ibid.

Von Spakovsky, who came to be known as "Hans von Redistricting," or HVR for short, was voting counsel to the assistant attorney general in charge of the Department of Justice's civil rights division. In that role, he oversaw the department's voting section and became the point person for undermining the civil rights division's mandate to protect the voting rights of U.S. citizens.

He was, in short, a fox in the henhouse.

In the Texas redistricting case, Von Spakovsky hijacked democracy, although we Democrats wouldn't learn about the enormity of his role until we gained access in early December, 2005, to a previously undisclosed Department of Justice memo in early December 2005more than a year after the 2004 elections.

After the state of Texas's lawyers submitted the unprecedented mid-decade redistricting plan to the Department of Justice, as required by the Voting Rights Act, every single nonpartisan career attorney in the civil rights division rejected the new map as unconstitutional and in violation of the Voting Rights Act.

According to the seventy-three-page memo, dated December 12, 2003, and endorsed by six career lawyers and two analysts in the department's voting section, the redistricting plan illegally diluted Hispanic voting power in two congressional districts. It also said the plan eliminated several other districts in which minorities had had a substantial, though not necessarily decisive, influence on previous elections.

These Department of Justice lawyers also revealed that they had consistently contacted Republican legislators and other state officials in Texas as they were drafting the new congressional map to be sure the state officials were aware that it was discriminatory, compared with other options.

But Von Spakovsky overruled the entire nonpartisan team of

experienced voting-rights lawyers to see that the new plan won department preclearance in time for the 2004 elections. The Supreme Court eventually would side with the judgment of the nonpartisan lawyers that portions of the plan violated the voting rights of Hispanics. The Department of Justice never should have cleared it.

Texas wasn't the only state HVR was screwing up. He was a mighty busy partisan manipulator.

He cleared a discriminatory voter identification and proof of citizenship law for Arizona—again over the unanimous determination of the career staff that the law would adversely affect Hispanic voters.

Von Spakovsky knew that in Arizona, as in Texas, Hispanic voters overwhelmingly cast their ballots for Democratic candidates. So, his partisan response was to erect obstacles to Hispanic political participation.

Mining a Republican-sponsored voting bill passed by Congress in 2002, the so-called Help America Vote Act, HVR instituted in a number of states dubious computer voting systems that lacked auditing provisions but included multiple voter identification provisions.

He actively perpetuated the political lie that voting fraud was rampant in the United States and used that excuse to find new and clever ways to diminish the role of minority voters. He violated a long-held tradition of the voting rights section of the Department of Justice against issuing advisory election opinions by sending out a series of letters to state election officials.

The letters had the effect of prompting states to implement the Help America Vote Act in exceedingly restrictive ways. One letter even advocated keeping eligible voters off voter rolls because of typos and other mistakes by election officials. When the state of Washington followed his advice—issued in the form of a partisan diatribe that he called an "opinion"—the federal courts struck down the action.

In the 2004 presidential election, HVR broke with established Department of Justice policy by getting involved with partisan litigation on the eve of the election. He drafted legal briefs in lawsuits between the Republican and Democratic parties in three battleground states—Ohio, Michigan, and Florida—and favored the Republicans' position in each.

In 2005, Von Spakovsky demanded that some states purge their voter lists. A federal court threw out that complaint, holding that there was no evidence of voter fraud or that any voter had been denied the right to vote. Even before joining the Justice Department, HVR had been a longtime advocate—through his testimony and writings—of restrictive voter identification laws. He believed that his native state, Georgia, had a problem with ineligible voters—although there was no data to indicate that—and pushed for a law that would require voters to provide multiple forms of identification.

In 2005, during the Department of Justice's review of the Georgia voter ID law, he not only failed to recuse himself from the case, but he also took over the management of the review process. Just before the review began, he even wrote an article in a Texas law review journal advocating restrictive ID laws, even though it was unethical for a Department of Justice official to weigh in publicly on a matter before the agency. Incidentally, he used a pseudonym, rather than his real name, on the article.

As in the Texas redistricting case, the nonpartisan career lawyers in the civil rights division concluded the Georgia voter ID law violated the Voting Rights Act. But Von Spakovsky once again overruled them and saw that it won the agency's approval. The law later was struck down by a federal court, which found that it harmed the voting rights of African Americans.

The Bush administration and its decision-makers at the "Just Us Department" went merrily along with Von Spakovsky's partisan spree, caring not one whit what its bleeding of American voting traditions had wrought.

In December 2005, Bush even nominated Von Spakovsky to the Federal Election Commission (FEC). Bush then gave him a recess appointment to an FEC vacancy in January 2006, allowing Von Spakovsky to take a seat on the commission while awaiting Senate confirmation.

But Democratic members of Congress—including then senator Barack Obama of Illinois—mounted a strong attack against confirmation with letters, phone calls, and committee testimony. With Senate Democrats still blocking his confirmation, Von Spakovsky had to leave the FEC when his recess appointment expired at the end of 2007. Whatever he is doing now, we all can rest a little more comfortably knowing he is no longer on the FEC.

* * * *

As noted earlier, Democratic congressman Ciro Rodriguez was unseated by a more conservative Democrat, Henry Cuellar, in the 2004 party primary. Democratic incumbent Chris Bell lost his primary race to Democratic challenger Al Green, an African American, in a new district designed to favor a black challenger. Democratic incumbent Jim Turner's district had been so torn apart that the eight-year congressional veteran didn't seek reelection.

Incumbent Democrats Frost, Stenholm, Sandlin, and I gave it our best shots in heavily Republican districts but lost to Republican opponents. The losses of Frost and Stenholm were difficult to bear, since each had contributed invaluable service to Texas during twenty-six years in Congress.

The new map prompted Ralph Hall to switch parties and win reelection as a Republican. Of the targeted Democrats, only Chet Edwards, Lloyd Doggett, and Gene Green survived without switching parties.

Doggett had to do most of his campaigning in South Texas, along the Mexican border, about three hundred miles from his home base in Austin. In their unsuccessful effort to remove Doggett from Congress, the Republicans had divided Austin into three congressional districts. They made Doggett's old District 10 a Republican district stretching east to the western Houston suburbs. A new District 25, which included Doggett's liberal Democratic voter base, reached across much of South Texas, all the way to McAllen. It was heavily Hispanic and designed to replace Doggett with a Hispanic Democrat. But Doggett hit the road, campaigned vigorously, and beat a Hispanic opponent in the Democratic primary. After the 2004 election, the district was redrawn by the federal courts leaving it a heavily Hispanic district but pairing it with San Antonio which was much closer to Austin than McAllen is.

My 2004 opponent was Ted Poe, a longtime felony district court judge in Harris County (Houston). It was a heartbreaking loss, my 43 percent to Poe's 55 percent. Although Jefferson County, my home county, gave me a 72 percent majority, I was swamped in the now larger and heavily populated Harris County portion of the district, which supported Poe with 70 percent of its vote.

This also was a presidential election year. Republican George W. Bush was seeking reelection against Democrat John Kerry at a time when opposition to the war in Iraq was growing, following the public disclosure that the administration had been wrong about Iraq hiding weapons of mass destruction.

Not only did we Democratic congressmen from Texas have to run in districts that had been designed to assure our defeat, we also had to contend with the Republicans' success in co-opting many of the fundamentalist churches as an arm of the GOP. Yes, churches, another surprise I should have seen coming.

In churches all over the country—including churches in Jefferson County—men of faith exhorted congregants to vote for Bush and, in many cases, Republican congressional candidates. They were free to do that. But when they told the faithful that they would go to hell for voting for John Kerry—or any other Democrat—they galloped across the line of propriety and the Constitution.

That's a subject worthy of whole libraries of other books. But to me, the most insidious part of the Republicans' courting of religion was their co-opting the churches for political money, especially when you consider Jesus's instruction for His church not to be part of any government.

* * * *

Texas Democrats lost six U.S. House seats in the 2004 elections. But Democratic congressmen weren't the only losers in the redistricting drama. The whole state of Texas lost.

Texas lost—in Martin Frost, Charlie Stenholm, and Jim Turner—the top spots on powerful House committees. Frost had been the top Democrat on the Rules Committee and would have been chairman when power shifted back to the Democrats.

Stenholm was next in line to be Agriculture Committee chairman, and Turner would have been the next chairman of the Homeland Security Committee.

All those powerful committees within a few years would have been led by Texans, were it not for the boneheaded move by Texas Republicans to dilute our state's influence over national policy in order to feed their own partisan greed. Texas lost much of its influence over national politics.

The districts of experienced, effective members of Congress had been radically altered to elect Republicans, rookie Republicans who landed at the bottom of Washington's pecking order.

As I noted earlier in this book, the Texas congressional delegation had been among the strongest of any state. When an issue important to Texas was on the line, everyone got behind it, Democrats and Republicans alike. The delegation had held regular bipartisan meetings so that each member could share the priorities and needs of his or her constituents with colleagues from across the state and receive their help.

Redistricting pretty much ended that practice. Members of the Texas delegation stopped attending bipartisan meetings. Republicans and Democrats mostly stopped talking with one another. Civility essentially was gone. I heard stories of members of one party checking the schedules of members of the other party to avoid even being on the same airplane. Another childhood lesson: If you can't talk to one another, you can't work together to solve the problems you face.

The new redistricting scheme also destroyed longtime communities of interest in Texas, robbing thousands of Texas voters of congressmen they had long supported and reducing their ability as citizens to influence decisions important to them and their neighbors.

That is what happened to Jefferson County and my hometown of Beaumont. Their influence in Washington was diminished by rabid partisan politics.

Under the Republican redistricting plan, Jefferson County and Beaumont were redrawn into a congressional district that was weighted by Houston, one hundred miles away. "Weighting" a district means to put the largest part of the population in one location to overwhelm a portion of the population somewhere else.

In the case of my new, drastically altered district, voters in suburban Houston now elect Beaumont's representative in the U.S. House, although the two cities don't always have common interests.

In fact, there are hundreds of issues large and small that would help Beaumont economically but cost Houston, and Ted Poe—DeLay's preordained Republican congressman—will show up first for Houston. It's an easy political decision to make for a Houston representative elected by port and energy interests. Some of those decisions are transportation/port infrastructure related, all of which weigh heavily on economic development that is leaving Beaumont for Houston.

The differences between the dominant Kingwood area of suburban Houston and the diminished area of Jefferson County in the new Second Congressional District are significant. Kingwood is a mostly retail and bedroom community of white-collar workers who commute into the Houston financial and medical centers. Beaumont and nearby Port Arthur are home to the workers who operate the huge petrochemical facilities up and down the Sabine-Neches waterway. What does either have in common with the other? Not much.

Jefferson County, with Beaumont and Port Arthur, always has been considered a centerpiece of an identified standard metropolitan statistical area (SMSA). Television stations in

Beaumont serve that SMSA of more than half a million people. But voters in Jefferson County now have less say over federal legislation affecting their future, and Beaumont has lost some of its identity to Houston.

The 2004 election outcomes were precisely what the Republican redistricting plan had been designed to do. But when elected officials pick voters—rather than voters picking elected officials—democracy is corrupted and neutered.

Tom DeLay didn't give a rat's tail about the health of democracy. For him, democracy was what suited his needs—and those of the Republican Party in the U.S. House of Representatives. It was a wholesale disruption of our concept of the sacred democratic philosophy: one person, one vote. And it was highly unconstitutional.

For the most part, DeLay's redistricting scheme had worked. But his overreaching soon would land him in legal and political trouble.

And for all the political disruption he and other Texas Republican leaders had imposed upon the state's voters, the new plan would enable the GOP to maintain control of the U.S. House for only one more election cycle. Remarkably, Democrats would recapture the House majority in 2006.

FOURTEEN

MELTING DELAY'S WINGS

Tom DeLay's obsession with his own power became so virulent that he saw himself as above the law, and in one incident in Washington, he demonstrated that mind-set in no uncertain terms.

One night at the famed Ruth's Chris Steak House in the capitol city of Washington, DC, DeLay wanted to finish off his lobbyist-purchased meal with a cigar. When reminded by the restaurant staff that federal law made it illegal to smoke in a public building, such as the restaurant, DeLay arrogantly and loudly replied, "I am the federal government!" This was politics at its worst.

The absolute worst, though, occurred on November 22, 2003, when the House of Representatives voted on a Medicare bill—and hit its lowest point during my tenure.

The bill was supported by DeLay and the Republican leadership but opposed by most Democrats—because we believed it didn't do enough for the Medicare program—and by some Republicans, including Congressman Nick Smith of Michigan, who thought it was too expensive.

After a long day and evening of debate, the vote was called about 2:00 a.m., and the bill failed by two votes. But the Republican leadership held the voting machine open and went to work. Around the House floor, small groups, or pods, of people started forming, and in each pod there was a wayward Republican being coaxed or browbeaten—maybe even being bribed—by the leadership to change his or her vote. The Speaker, Dennis Hastert, the majority leader, DeLay, and others were moving around, corralling members who they thought were the best prospects.

Three hours later, at about 5:00 a.m., there were a flurry of vote changes, and a single rap of the Speaker's gavel signaled that the bill had passed. It was hard for me to believe what I had just witnessed—the ham-handed manner in which people were cajoled and strong-armed into changing their votes, and I felt dirty when the night was finally over. The House had just approved a health-care bill that would not make life better for the average American but would benefit a handful of special interests, including the insurance and pharmaceutical industries. My side had lost on politics, not merit, and we lost a vote that we felt we had won— before strong political pressure was applied on the special interests' behalf. The experience left me wondering if that was going to be the way all votes in Congress were to be in the future. And it made it difficult for me to face my constituents back home.

Representative Smith, who was retiring at the end of that term, later would allege that DeLay had promised him he would endorse Smith's son in a state repesentative race in Michigan if Smith would change his vote on the Medicare bill. The congressman also said he was offered $100,000 for his son's campaign.

Overreaching can crush your dreams. Like the mythical Icarus, DeLay was flying too high and too close to the sun—on borrowed wings. Those wings soon would melt, and he would fall from grace with a magnificent crash.

* * * *

In the fall of 2004, only a few weeks before the new redistricting map would produce several new Republican congressional victories in Texas, the House ethics committee—in two separate decisions only days apart—slapped DeLay for unethical behavior.

On September 30, the committee admonished DeLay for improperly trying to win Nick Smith's vote on the Medicare bill by promising to support Smith's son in the state representative race. "The promise of political support for a relative of a member goes beyond the boundaries of maintaining party discipline, and should not be used as the basis of a bargain for members to achieve their respective goals," the the House Ethics Committee said.[38]

The panel, however, disputed the claim that Congressman Smith was offered $100,000 for his son's race.

Then, on October 6, the same committee—in a unanimous vote of its five Republicans and five Democrats—admonished DeLay for asking the FAA to track Pete Laney's airplane to Ardmore during the redistricting fight the previous year.

The committee's report cited House rules prohibiting members from taking "any official action on the basis of the partisan affiliation…of the individuals involved." It said DeLay's role in the incident "raises serious concerns under these standards of conduct."[39]

It was the third time that the committee had reprimanded DeLay for breaking House rules. In 1999, he had been rebuked for threatening to retaliate against a trade group that had hired a Democrat as its main lobbyist.

---

38   Letter to Hon. Tom DeLay from House Committee on Ethics, Rep. Joel Hefley et al, October 6, 2004, ethics.house.gov.

39   Ibid.

But the majority leader was defiant, responding that the complaint involving the redistricting fight "should have been thrown out immediately."

"For years Democrats have hurled relentless personal attacks against me, hoping to tie my hands and smear my name," he said. "All have fallen short, not because of insufficient venom, but because of insufficient merit."[40]

DeLay also saw to it that Representative Joel Hefley, Republican of Colorado, the independent-minded ethics committee chairman, was demoted for daring to speak truth to power, for daring to slap the wrist of the hand that held the hammer.

The Bush administration's Department of Justice straddled the political fence. It investigated DeLay for alleged money laundering for transferring cash to Republican legislative candidates in 2002, but it never brought charges.

The Department of Justice also investigated DeLay's relationship with disgraced lobbyist Jack Abramoff but cleared DeLay of any criminal violations in that case as well. Two former aides to DeLay, however, were among several people convicted in a bribery scandal involving Abramoff. And Abramoff served time in federal prison after pleading guilty to charges of conspiracy, tax evasion, and mail fraud.

Back in Texas, in the days after the 2004 election, Travis County district attorney Ronnie Earle stepped up his state investigation of DeLay's fund-raising activities, which had proved so important to the Republican takeover of the Texas House. And, in October 2005, DeLay and two associates—political consultants Jim Ellis and John Colyandro—were indicted by a Travis County grand jury for conspiracy and money laundering. They were

40   "House Ethics Committee Admonishes DeLay Again", CNN Washington Bureau, Oct. 7, 2004, CNN.com

charged with using DeLay's Texans for a Republican Majority PAC (TRMPAC) to illegally funnel $190,000 in corporate money to Republican legislative candidates.

Ellis ran DeLay's main national fund-raising PAC, Americans for a Republican Majority, and Colyandro was the former director of TRMPAC.

All three defendants pleaded not guilty—DeLay denounced Earle as an "unabashed partisan zealot"[41]—and spent the next several years fighting the validity of the indictments in court. The conspiracy indictment was thrown out, but the money-laundering indictment was still pending against DeLay in late 2010.

Under House rules, the indictment required DeLay to step down as majority leader. House Republicans softened the blow somewhat by giving DeLay a coveted seat on the Appropriations Committee, which had been left vacant when Randy "Duke" Cunningham, a California Republican, resigned after pleading guilty to taking $2.4 million in bribes from military and other government contractors.

Sadly, DeLay and Cunningham were but the tip of the iceberg in a jaw-dropping amount of indictments and federal investigations of Republican members of the U.S. House during those years.

Even sadder than the convictions that followed the indictments and investigations. Cunningham went to prison. Tom DeLay was convicted and sentenced to three years in prison, but after court hearings and appeals Tom DeLay's convictions were ultimately dropped. He never went to prison and was never punished for the crimes that he had committed, even though he paid a fine to the Federal Election Commission for the same charge on which he had been indicted and convicted in Texas. I was always disappointed

41   Jeffrey Smith, "DeLay Indicted in Texas Finance Probe," *Washington Post.*, September 29, 2005.

with the message that was sent to politicians who choose to push the envelope of the law while claiming to be acting in the best interest of the public.

It can also be noted here that years later in 2017, Steve Stockman, against whom I ran and defeated in 1996 and for whom Tom DeLay had raised a large amount of illegal campaign money, was hauled off in shackles from the airport in Houston, where he was trying to board a plane to Dubai. He was arrested and indicted for political corruption and misusing $350,000 he had raised in campaign funds. I am convinced his penalties will be severe, and I sincerely hope that DeLay and other politicians who play loose with the public's trust and money will always be caught and punished. Bad actors should never be allowed to even appear to be winners, because they aren't.

* * * *

After losing the 2004 election, I went home to play with my grandchildren and help some friends with their small businesses. I also looked forward to having dinner at home with my wife on a regular basis.

I had had a good ride in politics. I had started running for elective office right out of college. By 2004, I had been an active candidate for thirty-four years and had held office for twenty-nine of those, including the last eight in Congress. It seemed like it was time to go home and rest a little.

But it wasn't long before some of my friends started urging me to run for Congress again. And then I got a call from Rahm Emanuel (D-Il), then chairman of the Democratic Congressional Campaign Committee, asking me to consider running against DeLay in his

Houston-area district in 2006. Rahm would later would become President Obama's White House chief of staff and even later the mayor of Chicago, Illinois. I don't think he understood the personal and family sacrifice he was asking me to make. He convinced me, though, that this race could be the catalyst that could help begin to change the course of the Republicans' scorched-earth politics. DeLay had not yet been indicted by the state of Texas, but talk of the investigation of his actions, his aides, and of his relationship with Jack Abramoff was all leading to much talk and speculation that he might be in trouble.

Rahm felt that if a strong Democratic opponent could keep DeLay busy with his own reelection race at home, he wouldn't have much time to meddle in other important House races around the country. DeLay's absence could help the Democrats win some of those hotly contested races and possibly regain control of the House, he believed.

And, who knows? With a little luck, I might even win. DeLay seemed to be stepping in cow manure wherever he went. Despite (and partly because of) his redistricting success, his legal and ethical problems were mounting, and his unpopularity in Texas was growing.

I was torn about whether to run. DeLay was vulnerable. But challenging him seemed almost like playing the Republicans' game by running in a weighted GOP district. And how would another political race affect my family, especially my wife, Susan?

Susan is an amazing person and an unbelievably dedicated mother, grandmother, wife, and special education teacher, retiring after building a wonderful reputation among teachers and the families of the children whose lives she touched. I knew she most certainly would not be excited about the thought of more campaigning, more fund-raising, more travel, and more time separating me from her and our family. And that's being diplomatic.

Being a congressional spouse is a monumentally difficult task, maintaining a family and household pretty much on your own. This race would be even tougher than normal, and my previous congressional races had been vicious. I would be running against a "hammer," one who consistently fought dirty and dishonorably.

Remembering my family and our dedication to service, my choice was made. The easy thing to do—the lucrative thing to do—would have been to walk away. The right thing to do—the hardest thing to do—was to get back in the fight. And I was soon all in the fight.

I remembered Jimmy Stewart's Mr. Smith Goes to Washington character, who is asked why anyone should bother to fight a hopeless cause. Stewart's character, his voice straining from hours of uninterrupted speaking on the Senate floor, answered, "The only causes worth fighting for are the lost causes."

So I was back in it. Telling Susan was not easy, but our common pursuit of a greater good made her look at the mission with new eyes. And she knew we had ended the last election cycle in a way that was unsatisfying—to put it mildly.

* * * *

The day I announced my quixotic challenge of Tom DeLay, I received an unusual phone call from retired Republican congressman Dick Armey, the Texan and former house majority leader who had helped DeLay and Newt Gingrich destroy bipartisanship in the House only a few years earlier before falling out with the GOP leadership.

Armey called to thank me for running against DeLay. He told me that DeLay had done great damage to Texas's representation in

Congress. He also told me he would deny knowing me if I ever told of his call.

Armey's call stunned me. It helped me a lot to know that even some other Republicans got it. They knew the monumental damage that DeLay had done to Texas and the nation by engineering a partisan redistricting plan that removed many years of effective experience and leadership from the U S House of Representatives.

Republicans in 2006 held a 231–201 majority in the House, which meant that Democrats needed to win only sixteen seats to regain control. The extreme "Perrymandering" in Texas made the Democrats' challenge nearly impossible, even in a year when national political trends favored us. But I was a serious opponent for DeLay. The district was familiar to me because much of it had been part of the district I had represented for eight years before it had been eliminated by the 2003 redistricting map. Also, it encompassed the area where my grandparents had settled when they came to America from Sicily and I had many relatives living in the district.

The response to my new campaign was unlike anything I had ever experienced in politics. I enjoyed a magnificent groundswell of grassroots support, with people offering remarkable amounts of their time and money to help my campaign. Eighty-seven families invited me into their homes and had their neighbors come over to talk about what was important in their communities and what Congress needed to do to help. The campaign had 1,600 volunteers spreading the word that our corner of Texas didn't have to have political business as usual.

Those citizen patriots, Democrats and Republicans, knew that a trip of one thousand miles begins with a single step. Changing one member of Congress was the first step toward recreating the civility, the search for a common ground, that had built Congress into a once-great deliberative body.

Those citizens were on the right side of history. Tom DeLay was on the wrong side, declaring infamously in his last floor statement in 2006, "What we need in this Congress is more partisanship and less compromise."[42]

My campaign became the antithesis of DeLay's win-at-any-cost "theology", and it clearly was resonating with the people he purported to represent. In truth, the only interests he now represented in Congress were those of the national Republican Party and his corporate donors.

By mid-December of 2005, polls were showing that DeLay, now under indictment in Austin in connection with his fund-raising activities for Republican legislative candidates in 2002, was running behind in his reelection bid. My grassroots efforts were paying off, and people were becoming more disappointed and vocal about DeLay's push-the-envelope-of-the-law antics. DeLay also was under federal investigation for his involvement with Jack Abramoff, the disgraced lobbyist who was on his way to jail.

I spent a lot of time capitalizing on DeLay's notoriety, and I was successfully raising money. By February of 2006, I had $1.29 million on hand, very close to DeLay's $1.44 million. DeLay clearly was feeling the heat of an approaching political defeat, although it is hard to say whether it was feeling the heat—or seeing the light—that soon would determine his course.

He also was challenged in the Republican primary, which he won with more effort and money than a longtime incumbent should have expected to exert and spend. Although he was never short on

---

42   "Compromise DeLay-ing the Inevitable," Zack Smith, January 31, 2011, Alligator.org

cash, his legal expenses were beginning to eat into his fund-raising efforts.

By April, things were no better for him, and they were looking awfully good for me—in the district that DeLay had drawn for himself.

As his legal problems mounted, I moved ahead of DeLay by eight points in tracking polls, which indicated a large number of voters undecided. I was benefiting from his monumental negatives, but I never had to point them out.

"I have the luxury of being able to concentrate on issues like health care, immigration, and refinery safety," I told the newspapers. "I can say I'm going to be making headlines for the right reasons. I don't have to concentrate on what he did wrong, because that's showing up in the headlines in story after story after story."

When he realized he could not win, DeLay did what came naturally for him. A coward to the end, he tucked tail and ran by announcing that he would resign, effective in June 2006.

Surprisingly, my campaign staff and I were disappointed, rather than elated, because we had wanted to savor the satisfaction of beating him in the general election.

There was speculation in political circles that federal prosecutors "traded" DeLay's resignation for their decision not to bring federal criminal charges against him in connection with his 2002 fund-raising practices. The state criminal charges, however, remained.

DeLay's resignation should have been the end of the 2006 election story. But it wasn't because Republican Party bosses tried to force a replacement for DeLay onto the ballot, even though Texas law clearly stated that he was the eligible nominee, the only Republican name to legally appear on the ballot.

True to his character, DeLay tried to find a way around the law and announced he was moving to Virginia. He claimed his longtime Washington, DC–area condo as his homestead, and he changed his voter registration to Virginia.

The Texas Democratic Party then went to court and proved that DeLay and his followers were trying to manipulate the intent of the law. After a series of challenges and appeals, every court, nearly all dominated by Republican-appointed judges, ruled in favor of the Democrats' argument that DeLay's name could not be replaced on the general election ballot.

The jig finally was up when the highest court in the land, the U.S. Supreme Court, through Republican-appointed justice Antonin Scalia, also upheld the Democrats' position. You knew the sands were shifting when even Justice Scalia would no longer let Tom DeLay get away with his arrogant belief that he was "the law." Or, maybe that was precisely why he ruled that way. In our country, no one man or woman is "the law."

FIFTEEN

SUCCESS IS THROUGH THE MIDDLE

On June 29, 2006, the U.S. Supreme Court upheld most of DeLay's redistricting plan, but it found that it had unconstitutionally diluted the voting power of Hispanics in the vast Southwest Texas district held by Republican representative Henry Bonilla, as Hispanics did not traditionally vote for him.

The high court ruling didn't affect my race against DeLay, but it produced another upheaval in Texas's electoral politics because the boundaries of some other congressional districts were back in the hands of a three-judge federal panel—only a few months before Election Day. And Republicans—for a change—were on the redistricting hot seat. Proposed maps flew like a blizzard around Capitol Hill and Austin.

The House Republicans from Texas asked for a meeting with the Texas Democrats to try to agree on a map that would preserve the existing districts for both parties. The Democrats weren't about to get into bed with the wolves who had only recently devoured several of their colleagues, but they were curious and figured a meeting would at least be entertaining.

So, a meeting was held in the Speaker's Dining Room in the Capitol in Washington, while staff members stood together uncomfortably outside the room.

In a personal conversation with congressional staffer Cathy Travis, longtime adviser to Democratic representative Solomon Ortiz of Corpus Christi, the new "dean" of the Texas delegation in the wake of the recent losses of Martin Frost and Charlie Stenholm, Travis told me she approached a Republican staff member and asked, "So? What kinda map are they (Republicans) talking about?"

The rather junior GOP staffer described the map as one that was "fair to all the members." He said that if the Democrats and Republicans all agreed on the map being proposed—an impossibility—then the governor, the attorney general, and the Speaker of the Texas House, all Republicans, would ask the federal judges to adopt it as the new redistricting plan for South Texas.

"The governor, the attorney general, the speaker—they all gave their word of honor they'd all support this map," the staffer huffed importantly.

"Just so you know," Travis responded evenly, "all through this redistricting crap, anytime the governor, the AG, the speaker—any of the Republicans—gave their word, publicly or privately, they never kept it.

"Never," Travis emphasized. "Not a single one of 'em...not a single time. What's the definition of insanity? It's doing the same thing over and over and expecting different results."

The federal court made significant changes in the South Texas map, which resulted in Bonilla, the Republican incumbent, being unseated by Ciro Rodriguez, the former Democratic congressman from San Antonio who had been targeted by DeLay. Democrat Henry Cuellar of Laredo kept his seat, and Democrat Lloyd Doggett's District 25 no longer stretched three hundred miles from Austin to the Mexican border. Austin was still divided among three congressional districts, but Doggett's district was made more compact, and he was reelected.

* * * *

In my race, the only choice remaining for Texas Republicans trying to pick up the pieces of DeLay's destructive efforts was to try to unify around a write-in candidate against me. They were sure that a Democrat like me couldn't win in a 67 percent Republican-voting district, even against a write-in candidate.

But, fortunately, the moderate, independent Republicans were just as fed up with division and gridlock as the rest of us, and I was confident that many of them would turn out to vote for me in order to send that message. We, the people, Democrats and Republicans alike, were ready for a change.

Finally, it was Election Day, 2006, time for all those volunteers to work their magic, do what citizens have done for ages and take back their country. They did what Democrats have always done best. They hit the streets, knocking on more doors than could be counted, calling more voters than could be imagined, and showing their support with signs, T-shirts, and handouts.

And they brought home a victory, restoring honor to the Twenty-Second Congressional District of Texas. I won with almost 52 percent of the vote.

It was one of the proudest moments of my life. Voters in the district—Republicans, Democrats, and Independents—were willing to gamble on me as the independent voice I promised to be in Washington, DC.

* * * *

Joining the class of freshmen in the 110th Congress in January 2007 was exciting. Even though I was going to be serving my fifth term, it was magical to be part of the class that had won back control of the U.S. House of Representatives for the Democratic Party.

I had hoped my race would inspire—and provide political cover for—every Democratic challenger in the country. If I could slay the dragon (in his own district) who had kept us down for so long, anyone could do it in any district. My hope prevailed. The new Democratic majority in the House was 233–198. The Senate was evenly split, 49–49, between Democrats and Republicans, but two independents caucused with the Democrats to give Democrats the leadership.

But our revelry and celebration were tempered by the reality that the Republican opposition was more than formidable in both houses. President George W. Bush also had found his veto pen and was willing to use it to prevent Democrats from leading America in a new direction.

Many of us moderate Democrats began to search for moderate Republicans. Too many of the proposed solutions before Congress were being pushed out to the extremes, and we knew it was past time for those solutions to be pulled back to the middle of the political spectrum.

I remembered the success we had had by creating the Congressional Caucus on Missing and Exploited Children during my first term in 1997 and how it had become the largest bipartisan, issue-based caucus in the House. If that kind of success could be realized once, it could be realized again. I reorganized the caucus with Steve Chabot, a Republican from Ohio, as one of my cochairs. Steve was a good representative and fairly moderate. (Unfortunately, his district was too Democratic for him to hold, and he would lose, just as I would, in the 2008 election.)

Several other members had the same concern for restoring civility to Congress. I befriended three moderate Republicans who were being shunned by their party colleagues because they wouldn't toe the party line on a particular vote their leadership wanted.

THE DEATH OF WASHINGTON'S DEMOCRACY?

Shortly thereafter, I found similar efforts underway by Steve Israel, a Democrat from New York, and Tim Johnson, a Republican from Ohio, as well as by Kansas Democrat Dennis Moore and Ohio Republican Joann Emerson. Israel had begun to call his group the Center Aisle Caucus and was planning meetings with bipartisan organizations.

Wayne Gilchrest, a Republican from Maryland, and I joined with the other four, and the six of us—three Democrats and three Republicans—agreed to become the cochairs of a combined bipartisan caucus. We adopted the name Center Aisle Caucus and decided that any House member who wanted to join had to bring a member of the opposite party with him or her into the membership.

The caucus would grow to fifty-six members during that term. It is not, however, as active as it had been, and many of the participants have left the House either voluntarily or through defeat. In a recent conversation with first term Democratic congressman John Adler of New York, when I asked him if he had joined the Center Aisle Caucus he explained that he could not join. When I asked why, his answer was that the Republican he asked to be his partner in the caucus was told he would be "primaried" if he joined. That meant the party leadership would find and support an opponent to the incumbent, thereby punishing him for not following the directions of the party. Clearly, the leadership does not want anything standing in the way of keeping all of the potential votes in line. It is my continued hope that there will be efforts in the future to change this attitude and to find and implement innovative ways to bring opposing members together for the good of the country.

Combined with other bipartisan efforts, the Center Aisle Caucus has the potential to bring greater change to Congress than almost any other effort on Capitol Hill. It could help make civility and respect the rule of the day. Those of us who organized the caucus recognized that we could not succeed by merely forcing through legislation. That top-down philosophy simply is not accepted by the vast majority of Americans, and it is not accepted by many members of Congress.

* * * *

In 2010, a thousand people from all across America and from all political stripes gathered in New York and founded a new movement called No Labels. They gathered around Mark McKinnon, who had worked in the Bush administration, and Nancy Jacobson from the Clinton administration. Their bipartisan interests were just like those of the Center Aisle Caucus, but they did not have to contend with special interests or leadership who would want to control their decisions or efforts. I believed in what they believed in, civility and the search for common ground, so I was in New York with them as that committed group set out to change America. It included people like Mayor Cory Booker, a Democrat from Newark, New Jersey who later became a distinguished U.S. senator, and Republican Ambassador Jon Huntsman who ran for president of the US. Both are outspoken policymakers inspiring civility and the search for common ground.

No Labels began to grow and sought to have one million followers within its first few years. From the beginning they asked members of Congress to break with tradition and mix up their seating. When possible, sit with someone from your opposing party. Next, No Labels called for a simple but important goal when Congress couldn't pass a budget. Their mantra became "No Budget, No Pay," and it began to catch on in Congress and in the public. It became law because of that pressure. It was, and is, working. In just a few years they called for members of Congress to concentrate on problem-solving and also started encouraging members of Congress to wear lapel buttons calling themselves "Problem Solvers."

The vision is catching on and part of the reason is people are beginning to be more than frustrated with the gridlock and anger that is shutting America down. These actions show clearly that "We, the People" can make a difference and have our voices heard.

There must be a feeling of participation—both in Congress and in communities across the country—a feeling that every voice is being heard, even if it doesn't win every point of interest.

The Founding Fathers envisioned a deliberative body willing to respect differences, willing to compromise, and able to come to conclusions acceptable to a broad and diverse group of Americans. However, many people believe that Congress is no longer able to deliberate. That's not true because there still are members, although not enough, who understand—and practice—the art of compromise.

In the autumn of 2008, several colleagues and I were on the House floor, listening to a debate about energy. But it was more about finger-pointing than seeking a middle ground. Every Democrat who spoke blamed Republicans for the high cost of oil and gasoline and sought bans on drilling in Alaska and off the coastline around the nation. Every Republican blamed the Democrats for energy problems and insisted that more drilling was the only way to address the energy crisis.

Some of us not in the debate started to ask one another, "We know what the problems are, but what are the solutions?" A few hours later, about twenty-five of us gathered in a room to discuss solutions without assigning blame.

There were no lobbyists in the room, no committee staff, no

leadership, just members of Congress, with an aide or two to help with research and crunching numbers. The group was almost evenly divided between Democrats and Republicans, with maybe a few more Republicans. No one spoke about parties. We just stuck to the issue of energy.

Our goal was to try to come up with an energy plan around which we all could rally. That meant each of us would have to be willing to give up something we felt strongly about in order to win support for something others opposed. It became a remarkably comfortable give-and-take discussion that occasionally got a little boisterous. But we continued to stick by our original agreement, which was to stay in the room and work out our differences point by point on the issues that we wanted to be included in an energy bill.

This whole process, led by Democrat Neil Abercrombie of Hawaii and Republican John Peterson of Pennsylvania, took about six weeks. We came up with a seventy-five-page bill that all of us could understand and support.

We had respected one another and one another's ideas. No one got all he or she had wanted, but all were willing to support the effort to get an even-handed bill passed.

"Don't let the perfect be the enemy of the good" is a phrase applicable to passing legislation. In other words, if a bill is not that bad for your interests, but still isn't perfect in your eyes, don't vote "no" just because it isn't perfect. Negotiate and get an agreeable solution.

Everyone in our group was congratulating one another and remarking about how much fun we had had in getting the legislation drafted. "That's why I came to Congress, to participate in that kind of debate," a few were heard to say.

The attitude was markedly different from the drill-or-no-drill whining that had come from the far right and the far left during the earlier floor debate. America is a complicated nation, filled with people of many ideas and priorities. The solutions we sketched out on energy policy were in the gray area between the extremes.

A week after we finished our work, our bill had the support of about 150 members of Congress. It did not pass, but many members had found enormous satisfaction in working together without special-interest lobbyists and the heavy hand of our leadership.

If this experiment in bipartisanship finds any permanent success, it will be the personal highlight of my brief second-time service in the House of Representatives.

* * * *

My schedule as a congressman was tough. From the day I was sworn in, I was in a constant race to make floor sessions, committee hearings, and the myriad meetings my staff had scheduled for me—and to steal time to be with my family. Every day I had to campaign and raise money, every day I had to meet with constituents and give speeches, and every day I had to prepare for my next vote and my next interview. Thank goodness for my staff. They were amazing in their ability to screen the most important meetings for me and to see to it that I was ready to do what I needed to do—when I needed to do it.

My staffers were particularly crucial to me one Friday afternoon in March 2007, only a couple of months after my comeback election had returned me to Congress. The time seemed to be going by way too fast that day. I still had several votes to make on the Hill—including one key vote, the first effort to fund America's conflict in Iraq—meetings in the office, an airplane to catch, and a dinner to attend in Houston. I had already packed my bags and checked in online for my flight. My scheduler had printed my boarding pass and would have it ready for me with the weekend schedule and my reading materials when we left the office. I was hoping I would not have to rush to the airport, but it was looking like time would be tight.

One reason I was tight on time was because I had spent the early morning that day at the naval hospital in Bethesda, Maryland, following pains in my chest the night before. I had just failed a nuclear stress test, and the next thing I knew, the doctors were telling me I had to go into surgery because they had found a blockage in an artery. It could not be fixed with a stent and would require a bypass. They also were telling me it was hospital protocol to not allow me to leave but to perform the surgery right away. Were they kidding? I didn't have time for this!

I had a critical vote to make, a vote on the defense funding in Iraq, the first of the 110th Congress. The vote was to occur that afternoon, and I could not miss it. It was my job!

I called Dr. John Eisold, the chief physician for the House of Representatives. He was an admiral, and I knew he could override what the doctors were telling me at Bethesda. I had traveled with Dr. Eisold more than once and gotten to know him. A physician always accompanied members of Congress on official overseas trips. I could get Dr. Eisold to tell these doctors to let me come back to the Capitol for the vote. I had a friend, or so I thought. But he also told me to stay in the hospital!

Against his and the other doctors' advice, though, I put on my tie and left the hospital in Bethesda. Suzanne Jordan, my scheduler and office manager, was driving me back to the Capitol. Along the way, I called my wife, Susan, and a couple of my Houston friends,

Dr. Bernie Milstein and Dave Matthiesen, and asked them to find a heart surgeon for me. I called my office and canceled my appointments for the afternoon to make sure I could get on the Continental flight to Houston. I had to cast my important vote and then get home to an unknown ordeal. I wanted my family close by, not 1,200 miles away, when I had this surgery.

I made it back to my office and got organized to leave for what would probably be an extended absence. I told my staff to cancel that evening's dinner plans in Houston and be ready to cancel my entire schedule for the next several weeks, depending on what the doctors told me in Houston.

About that time my House pager went off, and bells started ringing all over the Capitol complex, telling me a vote had been called. I had fifteen minutes to get to the House floor. It was a series of votes, so I knew I would be in the Capitol for a while. I asked Suzanne, my trusted and always available staffer, to again be waiting for me in the car to take me to the airport as soon as the last vote was called. She would meet me outside the Capitol with the motor running to beat the crowd out of the parking lot, and then we would rush to the airport. We were used to the drill.

At the ten-minute warning bells, I decided to casually walk to the Capitol instead of running at the last minute, as I usually did, to make my votes. I didn't want to stress my body any more than necessary. Apparently, it already had been going through a lot of stress, which is probably what prompted the need for circulatory bypass surgery. I was not excited about this, to say the least.

I cast my votes and then told Speaker Nancy Pelosi and Majority Leader Steny Hoyer about my situation. They thanked me for making the important vote and, hugging me on the House floor, wished me well. We all had tears in our eyes.

I went to Dr. Eisold's office and asked him to talk with my new doctor in Houston. He did, and after the conference call, he and the other Capitol doctors gave me a bottle of nitroglycerine, which they cautioned me to keep handy on my flight to Houston...just in case I had more pain or a heart attack.

Suzanne was waiting for me as planned. Traffic between Capitol Hill and Washington National Airport was slow, but it was less congested than normal, and we didn't have to rush too much. I checked in, went through security, and straight to the plane.

When I got to my seat, I started thinking about all the things I had experienced during the previous ten years—my first congressional election; being sworn into one of the country's top offices; representing my country in places all over the world; trying to make friends for my issues of missing children and space exploration; working for civility in the House; fighting against the divisive Texas redistricting; votes on war, impeachment, budgets, and deficits; raising money for election after election; rushing from speech to speech and from neighborhood to neighborhood; living away from my family for most of the time; and much, much more. Could all that have contributed to my health problem? Probably! So why did I do it? I loved my work. I love my country.

I made it to Houston just fine. My friend and colleague, Mike Lykes, met me at the gate to make sure I was all right. He wanted to drive me to St. Luke's Hospital, but my car was at the airport. I told him I would drive and asked him to follow me. He did. Mike had taken care of me for years. He was my friend, my fund-raiser, my chief of staff for a while, and my adviser. Even though he had a sick child fighting cancer, he was there taking care of me. People don't come much better than that.

Being in the hospital gave me a lot of time to reflect some more on my life and my family. I thought about the situation in which I had put my family and friends by moving away from my lifelong home to try to help end the reign of terror Tom DeLay had wrought on Texas and on the U.S. House of Representatives. I thought of my twelve years of seven-day weeks, eighteen- to twenty-hour days, the stress of constant campaigning, the hell of redistricting, and all the nice people I just wanted to represent.

My surgery went well, thanks to a magnificent team of doctors that included Bud Frazier, Billy Cohn, and my new friend and cardiologist, Reynolds Delgado. What wonderful, talented people. All the nurses and professional staff in the Valentine ward at St. Luke's also were great. They told me I could go home after I completed a mile-long walk around the nurses' station. That was all I needed to hear...a challenge. On the morning of the Friday following the Sunday of the surgery I achieved my mile-long goal, and they sent me home...with my pillow, for those who belong to the zipper club.

Less than a week later, Mike had me back on the phone, talking to friends and constituents. Damn! I hate raising money. Every day of a politician's life, calls must be made to raise the money necessary to get reelected. Wouldn't it be nice if we could just be representatives for a while and do the people's work? Yes, it would.

I realized that all those days I had fretted over my future during the redistricting fight, my loss to Ted Poe in a district that was taken from the people of Texas's Golden Triangle, and my battle to stop the egregious actions of Tom DeLay, which I had internalized so strongly, had put me where I was—healing from major heart surgery.

But I was still a member of Congress, and I had work to do. I followed doctors' orders and took six weeks to recover. Then it was time to continue my work and try to keep the district I had taken from Tom DeLay. I had fought much too hard for the past two years to let it slip away without every ounce of fight I could muster.

* * * *

Early in 2008, Jeff Mosely, the chairman of the Greater Houston Partnership, approached me and made a passionate appeal about why the community needed me to stay in Congress.

"Your success is one of the most important tasks we face this year," he said. "We need good representatives with seniority again. We lost so many good representatives with so much seniority and leadership through redistricting that Texas is now losing important projects. It will be a shame if we lose your ten years of seniority and another chairmanship as well."

But my reelection effort in 2008 did not have a fairy-tale ending. Running on the DeLay-designed uneven playing field, I narrowly lost to a Republican rookie.

My loss was not a defeat of ideas, but the result of reality of a process that was beyond my control. Democratic representation in the United States was never meant to be preordained. Voters can only really affect change when the die is not already cast for one party or the other. I'd gotten a lucky break in 2006 when DeLay decided to flee the state and our election matchup.

The 2008 loss inspired me to be a full-throated advocate for the civility we need in Congress, as well as for the steps we need to take—in the state and local government and in Congress—to loosen the grip of partisanship.

* * * *

Again, I had reached a point in my life where I thought politics was over for me. The last time I had said I had done enough and wanted to go home and play with my grandchildren did not end up being fact; I just couldn't stay away. My friends have always told me that politics gets in your blood, and you can't get it out. Apparently, that's true. In 2009 when I finished my fifth term in Congress, moved everything back home to Beaumont, and rented out my house in Stafford. I joined my friend and former campaign consultant, Mustafa Tameez, in his public relations company, Outreach Strategists, Inc. We began soliciting clients and attempted to use the knowledge each of us had gained in our various experiences to be beneficial to our community. I was doing OK and staying busy enough and earning enough money to be able to pay Susan's and my bills. I did work for the city of Houston, the International Center for Missing and Exploited Children, the Association for Ambulatory Behavioral Healthcare, and others. This was plenty to keep me busy. My friends are correct, however, and I could not stay away from following the political actions of my great state of Texas.

Another round of redistricting occurred in 2010 and 2012, opening up what appeared to be an opportunity for a moderate Democrat possibly to win an open congressional seat, and it was where I lived in Beaumont. The district was drawn to perform at about 58 percent Republican. It was made less Republican because the Republican establishment was somewhat disenchanted with Congressman Ron Paul (R-TX) because of his renegade actions as a presidential candidate, and his support of Libertarian ideals and the Tea Party organization. When he announced he would not run, that left the seat open with no incumbent. They did not seem to care if he lost his race for reelection, and they pretty much knew whoever did win would be a Republican. When he announced he would not seek reelection, I immediately thought it might present an opportunity for me to return to Congress again.

I called some of my consultants together and decided to commission a poll to determine if there was an opportunity for a Democrat to win in this difficult district. We learned that I would do very well in my home county (I knew that) and that results in Galveston County were trending more Republican, but based on the results of earlier elections there, I should be able to show strongly enough in Galveston County that with support from my home county it was possible to win the race. It would be later that we would learn about the strength of the Tea Party and right-wing idealism becoming prevalent in northern Galveston County as people migrated out of Houston, fleeing the inner-city life and running to conservative suburbs. Northern Galveston County, and specifically League City, was one of the fastest-growing areas in the state. We also discerned that it would be a race that would cost well in excess of $2.5 million. We would have to be on the Houston TV, which is the fourth most expensive media market in the United States. We relied significantly on my strength with the space community in the hope that the employees of NASA living in this congressional district would remember the good work I had done and would support me for the work I would do on their behalf in the future. If I won this election I would be the first person in our history to win congressional races in three mostly different congressional districts. We knew it was a long shot. It was one, however, with which I was tempted to go forward.

Susan, my wife, was not happy, but she supported my decision as she always had and joined the effort to try to send me back to the House of Representatives. The race was difficult, as expected. It was almost one solid year of traveling, speech-making, fund-raising, and town-hall meetings. I won the endorsement of all of the major newspapers and was told that I "knocked it out of the park" with the one debate we had at the Clear Lake Country Club. My ads were working well in Jefferson County (my home county), but we had not yet reached the amount of money necessary to be on network TV in the Houston media market. The DCCC, who had been supportive, got cold feet at the end and did not give me the infusion of cash I hoped to have that would have put me on TV in Houston, and thus reach the people of League City. I think that hurt, but we were also learning that the attitude of the northern Galveston County area was showing huge conservative sentiment and tended to vote straight Republican even though it was not in their best interests. Tracking polls were showing enough strength for a victory all the way up to the end of the election. When the early vote was announced, we knew we were in trouble. I was able to call Randy Weber and concede the race to him fairly early in the evening. The race had been ugly and left a bitter taste in the mouths of my family, staff, and volunteers. It is always hard to lose, but when elections become personal, as this one had, the ill feelings linger. It's too bad, because that is not the way it has to be.

I was disappointed I did not win but pleased with my showing. I had made the race largely to send a message of moderation, attempting to promote civility and respect in debate and my feeling that there is common ground in every issue, no matter how difficult or far apart we may be in our beliefs. I am still convinced that idea will catch on and we will return to civility and compromise.

I still won't say I am through with politics. If Texas will change the way we draw boundaries for congressional districts and make them competitive, I will be right back in the game trying to take my message to Congress.

SIXTEEN

THE WAY FORWARD

We've reached meltdown in the United States—in our economy, in our national security, and in the composition of our government. Politically, we are in a state of dysfunction. And only we the people can put us back on the right track.

This is our common birthright declared in the Constitution, and it is our responsibility to exercise it. Each of us has a role to play in putting government back on a path that will accommodate a wide marketplace of ideas – a government that will focus on passing legislation to help the American economy and the American people, not prolong the agony of partisan gridlock.

The historic elections of President Barack Obama in 2008 and President Donald Trump in 2016 proved that most Americans want change in Washington, and it illustrated the power that the American people can harness. But that was just one step.

These presidential elections, unfortunately, did little to release the crippling grip of partisanship over Congress. It may even have tightened it, as demonstrated by the divisiveness over the president's efforts to win enactment of one of the signature issues of our time, something as basic as long-overdue health- care reform for our nation. After months of partisan strutting and sniping, a health-care bill finally won congressional approval only to be taken up again at the first change of partisan control. But not a single Republican in either the House or the Senate voted for its original passage and not one Democrat has opted for the most recently proposed changes—not one.

THE DEATH OF WASHINGTON'S DEMOCRACY?

Now, perhaps more than ever before, the public must get involved in the political process—and stay involved.

Before I go any further, though, let me make it clear that I am not talking about joining something like the anti-government Tea Party movement that started erupting around the country soon after President Obama was elected and helped propel President Trump into office. We can't move our country forward by marching behind an angry, tenuous alliance of anti-tax complainers, immigrant bashers, secessionists, anarchists, and simply frustrated but ill-informed people, who likely don't even know who their representatives in Congress are.

This is exactly what happened in the 2016 election. Angry people, not knowing where to turn, were drawn to the person who claimed that he alone could fix the problems that faced us in this country, in spite of not having any experience in government or any knowledge of the operations of our Congress. When Donald Trump was elected president of the United States, he carried the anger of the public into the White House and into Washington, DC, guaranteeing that the eight-year battle over health care would end with repeal, and the promise that the replacement would be made to be a beautiful system, cheaper and more accessible to more people. His predictions, however, have not yet borne the fruit expected by the people who had put their trust in him. That was just an indication of how difficult these matters of governing are and how sensitive change for the good of the people can be when we don't have compromise and a willingness to search for common ground. When we listen to one another with open minds, the suggestions we develop from the strengths of one another's words always yield greater solutions than those proposed by one single determined mind.

We need more citizen-patriots, people who may be unhappy with their government (many of you are, as am I) but want to work within the political system to improve it, not tear it down. We have to raise our voices, raise our hands, raise our awareness. New voters must get involved and stay involved. People need to tell their representatives in Congress: "You don't get to pick me; I get to pick you." Citizen patriots must have the confidence to express their thoughts, not the thoughts of professional opinion makers. We must promote a sense of unity as a part of making this participatory democracy work.

We must start by demanding two important remedies in establishing the membership of the U.S. House of Representatives.

First, we must demand that Congress take the power of redistricting the U.S. House and other political subdivisions away from partisan state legislators and require the states to appoint independent commissions to accomplish that crucial task. As I have noted in previous chapters, redistricting is a major factor in determining how partisan House districts—and their representatives—will become, and, consequently, how effective or ineffective those representatives will be in forging workable compromises to our nation's difficult, divisive problems. It is difficult, if not impossible, to remove all politics from the process, but if congressional campaigns are to be truly competitive and allow an opportunity for a moderate candidate to attract moderate votes from the opposing party, the effort must be made. There is no reasonable alternative.

Second, we must demand that Congress ban mid-decade redistricting, such as the Republicans imposed upon Texas voters in 2003, which then spread across the country in less than one decade. Without such a prohibition, there will be nothing to stop rabid leaders of either party from attempting power grabs at any time in other states, destroying communities of interest and dictating partisan terms to voters.

And just in case Congress is slow to act, we must demand that similar laws be enacted by legislatures on the state level.

Will these changes alone free Washington of its partisan shackles? Maybe not alone, but, honestly implemented, they will be major steps toward creating districts in which partisanship is not the overriding factor in electing members of the House.

To those who would argue that independent commissions wouldn't be any more successful than legislative bodies in creating more level playing fields for congressional elections, I would point out that they couldn't be any worse. And we will never know if we don't try. The point is, what we have now isn't working, and there is a viable alternative.

Six states—Arizona, Hawaii, Idaho, Montana, New Jersey, and Washington—already use independent, bipartisan commissions to draw their congressional lines. And Indiana uses a commission if the legislature fails to enact a redistricting plan.

Those states already are trying. So is Iowa, which doesn't have a commission but requires all congressional districts—as well as those for the Iowa House and state senate—to be drawn by nonpartisan legislative staffers without using any political or election data. They don't even have the home addresses of incumbents. They present the Iowa Legislature with a redistricting map on which to vote.

Several states, including California, also have independent commissions to redistrict their state legislative seats.

But most states, including Texas, still give their legislatures first shot at redistricting. Lawmakers usually grind themselves down by trying to please their parties and protect reelection prospects for their friends in Congress and, in many cases, trying to draw districts to maximize their own success were they ever to run for U.S. Congress. The redistricting effort often will disrupt or affect work on other important issues facing legislators.

Then, almost inevitably, someone—often several dissatisfied groups—will file lawsuits over the state legislature's product, leaving the final boundaries to be drawn by judges.

The Fifth U.S. Circuit Court of Appeals, in upholding the DeLay redistricting plan for Texas, warned that mid-decade redistricting created tremendous potential for abuse and strongly suggested that Congress prohibit it.

"Congress can assist by banning mid-decade redistricting, which it has the clear constitutional authority to do, as many states have done," the judges wrote.[43]

Unfortunately for good government, though, the U.S. Supreme Court held that a state can alter congressional boundaries anytime it pleased. The high court said that since redistricting is an inherently political endeavor, politics could drive the timing and frequency.

I believe that decision was so profoundly wrong that the Supreme Court, the next time it has a chance to answer the question, will reverse it. But we can't afford to wait. Our elected lawmakers must act now. We, the people, must act now!

Congress has the authority to give states the parameters to follow in carrying out congressional redistricting. In article I, section 4 of the Constitution, the framers gave Congress the power to enact laws governing the time, place, and manner of elections for members of the House of Representatives. And the Fourteenth Amendment gave Congress the power to enact laws to enforce the fair apportionment (redistricting) of its members. As the appellate court pointed out, Congress can instruct states to redistrict only once every ten years.

43   Ibid.

But even with all the potential benefits of making the changes, persuading Congress or state legislatures to create independent redistricting commissions and ban mid-decade redistricting won't be easy. Resistance will come from many lawmakers, particularly state legislators who want to run for Congress and want to have a chance to carve out friendly districts for themselves. Some party leaders may oppose change.

My former House colleague, John Tanner, a Democrat from Tennessee, in 2007 introduced a bill, the proposed Fairness and Independence in Redistricting Act, which would have banned mid-decade redistricting and required states to use independent commissions for redistricting.

The bill attracted a handful of sponsors but was never passed. Even if it had been passed by Congress, it probably wouldn't have been signed into law by then president George W. Bush.

In Texas, former state senator Jeff Wentworth, a Republican from San Antonio, and state representative Joe Deshotel, a Democrat from Beaumont, have tried unsuccessfully to create a nonpartisan commission to perform congressional redistricting and remove the political gyrations from the process. The bill, which has been introduced for several years now, never has advanced very far in the legislative process. It won committee approval in the Texas Senate in 2009 but failed to muster enough votes for full Senate action.

"Redistricting is a subject that can get lawmakers' blood boiling [and] their hearts racing," Senator Wentworth said in Texas Weekly in March 2009. "Unfortunately, Texas voters are less passionate about the redistricting process, showing little interest until the partisanship and fractiousness that always results during redistricting make headlines."

Wentworth added: "The last time Texas went through the redistricting process, the Texas Legislature became such a laughingstock that Jay Leno made jokes about it on TV. I don't want that to happen again."[44]

The legislator also cited the three-way division of Travis County that DeLay engineered in 2003 in an unsuccessful effort to defeat Democratic congressman Lloyd Doggett of Austin.

[45]"This three-way separation of a single community of interest was unfair to both Travis County residents and those who live in the other counties that make up the congressional districts," he said.

Separating communities of interest becomes a by-product of the partisan-driven legislative gerrymandering necessary to either get rid of a congressman from the minority party or protect incumbents from the majority party.

"Protected incumbencies discourage challengers. So voters' choices could be limited to a 'token' challenger or to no choice at all," Wentworth said.[46]

In other words, the community interests of the voters in a district are disregarded, if necessary, to promote partisan interests.

Wentworth's bill called for a commission of eight voting members—four Republicans and four Democrats, chosen by Texas legislators—and a ninth, nonvoting member. None of the members could be elected officials, major party officials, or registered lobbyists, and at least two of the eight voting members would have to be from counties with relatively small populations.

"I have no doubt that each of the parties will choose members

---

44   Jason Cohen, "Wentworth and Jones: Who's Suing Who?", *Texas Weekly Magazine*, March 2009.

45   Ibid.

46   Ibin.

whose loyalty to their respective political party is as strong as horseradish,"[47] Wentworth said, and I agree. The idea is to put equal numbers of partisans in a situation where compromise must occur, with any luck pulling the ultimate decisions over districts toward the middle of the political spectrum.

If together the partisans on a politically balanced redistricting commission can draw fair and legal congressional districts and decide on a map by majority vote, the potential benefits become obvious—less partisan bickering in Congress, more time for the business of government, a greater opportunity for civility and compromise on difficult issues, more campaign debate on the real issues, and less personal bashing between candidates.

I firmly believe that this would lead to higher voter turnout in elections because it would empower individual citizens to be a more effective part of the electorate.

Wentworth ended a long legislative career in late 2010 to take a job with Texas A&M University. Let us hope other Texas legislators will join state representative Deshotel in his continued promotion of the commission proposal.

Congress also has an opportunity to take the wheel and steer the whole country to a place where the process of dividing states into congressional districts is balanced and fair. Banning mid-decade redistricting and requiring all states to form transparent commissions to draw congressional boundaries around communities of interest could be the most important steps Congress has taken in generations to improve U.S. elections and representation in the U.S. House.

But Congress won't take those steps unless America—"We the People"—rises up and demands them.

---

47   Ibid.

The tsunami of things that are in crisis—our economy, our health care, our military, our foreign policy, the very earth beneath our feet, and dozens of other serious matters—will not be successfully addressed if lawmakers continue to snipe at one another over partisan differences.

It is up to us, the citizen-patriots, to demand change. We have to demand that Congress and state legislatures take the steps outlined here to create more fairly drawn districts, drafted around communities of interest, to see the level of debate in Washington rise. Heed George Washington's caution to not allow the rise of partisan power to be more important than Congress itself, take up John Kennedy's challenge of what you can do for your country, and realize that only through our individual actions, starting now, can the process of real change begin.

Only when consensus builders in individual congressional districts are the rule—not the exception—can Congress make informed decisions and enact creative policies to address the multiple challenges facing this nation and provide opportunity for all, not merely devise schemes for a few.

The need for this change is right now. Texas and other states will proceed with redistricting again at the end of this decade and each decade, and partisanship once again will largely drive the process. It is time now to lay the groundwork for doing it right.

As I pointed out earlier in this book, I grew up in a middle-class part of Beaumont, Texas. My family may not have had much, but we learned to protect one another's interests, to care about others, and to share and be responsible by planning for each next generation, not just for ourselves for today. The future is here now, and it is time to begin repairing our fractured America.

Members of our national family must share that same spirit with which I grew up in my family. It's the spirit of citizen-patriots. That's my America!

POSTSCRIPT

What can we do now?

End hatred! Teach tolerance! Encourage conversation within our places of worship, families, neighborhoods and communities. Teach ourselves to think for ourselves and stop tacitly accepting the opinions we now hear all around us. Teach basic civics and the lessons we learned from the studies and sacrifices made by our founding fathers and the myriad of citizen patriots who have tried for centuries to create a successful attempt at civilly governing ourselves. Teach that respect and open mindedness begins with me!

Write your representatives and express YOUR opinion. Understand the impact to our communities and the civility of our Congress when we allow government subdivision boundaries to be gerrymandered, and insist that your representatives vote accordingly. Promote ideas like redistricting commissions that will act with less partisanship than a legislature and support the candidates who seek to set aside partisanship. Stop voting by label! Consider joining the movement being promoted by No Labels. You can find it at (www.nolabels.org).

Visit these websites and share your views:

www.thedeathofdemocracy.com
www.changebeginswithme.biz
www.lampsonbooks.com

ABOUT THE AUTHOR

Nick Lampson, former U.S. Congressman, has acted in government for forty-two years, ten of those in the U.S. House of Representatives. His political saga started in local elected office and continued to numerous state agencies and committees, including Congressional Committees on Science, Space and Technology; Transportation and Infrastructure; and Agriculture. He created the Congressional Caucus on Missing and Exploited Children, helped create the Congressional Center Aisle Caucus, worked in Congress on science issues involving space, environment and energy and was a delegate to the NATO Parliamentary Assembly. He has been a high school science teacher, a university instructor, a community activist, legislator, lobbyist, family man and concerned citizen. Since congress he was appointed to a National Academies of Science study to modernize the National Weather Service and to serve as Chief Operating Officer of a healthcare delivery system in Southeast Texas.

ISBN 9780692934456

9 780692 934456 >